The Proper Care of Snakes:

Managing Personality Disorders in
Congregational Settings

Roger Kruger

ISBN:**0692356487**
ISBN 13: **9780692356487**
Grace Point Resources, Omaha, Nebraska
Scripture quotations, unless otherwise noted, are from the New
International Version, **THE HOLY BIBLE, NEW
INTERNATIONAL VERSION®, NIV® Copyright © 1973, 1978,
1984, 2011 by Biblica, Inc.® Used by permission. All rights reserved
worldwide.**

DEDICATION

To all those individuals with whom I have worked in counseling for helping me to grasp the manner in which individual personality provides a window on the world.

CONTENTS

ACKNOWLEDGMENTS

I am deeply indebted to intentional interim pastors Chip Borgstadt, Lowell Hennigs, Lynn Parsons, and Linda Walz for their assistance in compiling examples and to Don Tubesing for reviewing the manuscript and offering suggestions.

1 THE PROPER HANDLING OF SNAKES

You may have heard before the fable of the rattlesnake and the boy:

A boy was climbing a mountain when, near the top, he was startled to see a rattlesnake lying across the trail. The rattlesnake said to the boy, "It is cold here, and I am dying. Please pick me up and take me down the mountain with you."

The boy said, "But you are a rattlesnake. If I pick you up, you will bite me."

"No," said the rattlesnake. "I promise I will not bite you. Please take me down the mountain so I won't die."

The boy hesitated but finally relented, carefully picking up the snake. The snake seemed limp and helpless. He folded him inside his coat to warm him and began the trek back down the mountain.

At the bottom of the mountain, he took him out of his coat and set him on the ground, whereupon the snake bit him.

The boy cried out, "Mr. Snake, why did you do that? You promised not to bite me. Now I will die!"

The snake said, "But you knew that I was a snake when you picked me up."

I don't know what the original moral of the story was intended to be. Was it, "kill snakes whenever you have a chance" or was it, "whenever dealing with snakes, know how to handle them"?

I prefer the latter interpretation. Not all snakes are alike. Some are dangerous; some are not. It is useful to know the difference. And if you choose to pick up a snake and carry it—even one that is limp and about to die—you won't cradle it in the same way you would, say, a lamb: close to your chest.

Congregations include many different kinds of people and many different types of personalities. Too often the assumption is made everyone can be treated alike. That sometimes leads to hurt and amazement, as a vicious bite is the response to what we assumed was care and compassion. The snake is never amazed: "Didn't you know what I am?"

I knew almost nothing about personality theory when I accepted a call to serve an old and traditional congregation in the heart of a large city. Before my arrival, the congregation had undergone a split. My predecessor had encouraged relocation to the suburbs. Since the majority of the membership were families who commuted to the downtown location, to him it made sense that relocation would further the congregation's outreach to young families. He succeeded in getting the board of directors to agree to this move. Many, however—especially those with generational ties to the history of the congregation at that location—strongly resisted. The only solution appeared to be to create two congregations out of the one. Members were given the option of remaining with the congregation at the historic site or becoming part of the new congregation in the suburbs. With the traditional group bolstered by a sizable number of those who didn't bother to choose either way, the final division was about fifty-fifty.

Being rather young and naïve and seeing myself as a healer, I accepted a call to serve those who remained with the urban church. I sensed that the vision and goals of my predecessor were probably on target. However, the means he had used to accomplish those goals appeared to have been unnecessarily harsh and abrupt. I hoped that through listening, patience, and compassion, the remnant could eventually grow and become vital and alive once again, and I believed that with time they could rediscover a mission in their urban location.

My first couple of years there, I was engaged in something very much like grief counseling. The division of the congregation had split families and long-term friends. It didn't take much to cause the pain and loss to rise to the surface, and I heard the same stories repeated over and over. Anger at the previous pastor was a significant part of their grief. They were resentful and opposed to nearly everything he had attempted to do. Though I didn't always say so, many of the things they were critical of were things that I too might have proposed. But it was not time to argue about such things. Healing had to come first.

However, one of the things he had attempted to do, which seemed to have been the issue that finally coalesced all the opposition against him, puzzled me. He had attempted, I was told, to remove the organist and music director. One of the current congregational leaders informed me that he first became involved when he learned of it, boasting that because of his involvement, he had ultimately been the key figure in "getting rid of" their former pastor. While many of the former pastor's actions made sense in the light of congregational revitalization theory, deposing the organist did not. I was, in fact, quite pleased with her. Having previously served congregations that struggled with volunteer organists whose playing was often too slow or haltingly unpredictable, I was delighted to have one who was both an accomplished musician and able to play from the heart. She also appeared to have a devoted following among the choir (the congregational agitator being one of them).

She was a single woman in her midforties, who first began playing the organ as a teenager. She had lived a rather unpleasant childhood: she had been raised by a very demanding mother who used part of their home for taking care of aging adults with dementia. It was an environment that had its share of horror stories. Her mother had died before I had come on the scene, but when she talked about her, she described what a wonderful woman she had been—a description that didn't seem to match things I heard about her from others.

I wondered whether my predecessor perhaps thought it was merely time for a change, but still it seemed to me that the attempt to get rid of her was an arbitrary and risky strategy, likely to produce more damage than gain. No doubt, my opinion in this matter was further bolstered by the fact that she seemed pleased with my pastoral leadership and was often complimentary. I politely returned her compliments.

As time went on, however, I began to notice some peculiar things. For one, there always seemed to be some kind of problem hovering over the music program. The issues never seemed to be major ones; nonetheless, they tended to generate much heat and anger. People complained. People quit. I could never put my finger on the exact issue. There just seemed to be continual turmoil.

After my arrival, I attempted to hold staff meetings with both the full-time and part-time staff—something that hadn't been done before. She was an irregular attender, often showing up late or sometimes not at all, seldom contributing. It was clear that she didn't like things that were required of her.

Over a period of time, I noticed something else: she seemed to develop extremely intense friendships. Quite suddenly, overnight it seemed, a person became her best friend. They were seen everywhere together. They shopped together, went to restaurants together, and even vacationed together. And suddenly, just as quickly as it began, it came to an end, and they were no longer on speaking terms with one another.

Then one day a person told me that the organist was in love with the elderly retired pastor, who was a widower and served the congregation on a part-time basis making visits to the shut-ins. It was not just that she liked him and admired him; she planned to marry him. I laughed when I was told this, as it seemed the most unlikely of couples, he being nearly thirty years her senior. In time, though, I found that it was likely true. Though it was doubtful that the man in question was ever aware of it, she had confided her intentions to several of her friends.

This did indeed seem strange, but I figured that either she had just been joking about it and others had taken her seriously, or it had simply been the fantasy of someone who could at times be quite lonely.

I no longer remember what our first argument was about, but I remember the outcome. I went from being "the best pastor she had ever known" to the absolute worst. She stormed out of the office, slamming the door behind her. I didn't hear from her for a couple of days and wondered if maybe she was going to resign. However, she showed up for church again the next Sunday. Not only did she show up: she was again pleasant, as if nothing had happened between us.

After a while, I began to hear complaints that were directly at her. The most serious was that she was showing up at rehearsals with the smell of alcohol on her breath. I decided that was an issue I had to address. I knew that if I asked her to come to the office to meet with me, more than likely she would be suspicious and offer some excuse for not coming. I decided to drop by her house.

The confrontation, such as it was, went well enough. I dreaded confrontations and was fearful about how this would go. As it turned out, we ended up having a rather useful conversation about a variety of things. She denied the alcohol accusation, of course, but she didn't seem too angry about it. I hoped that at least if there had been a problem, having brought the issue out in the open, there would less likely be a repeat.

Later, I learned that she was telling others that I was attracted to her, as I had stopped by to see her at home when she was alone. I felt foolish for not realizing the danger that should have been obvious from her fantasy about the retired pastor. This was a woman, who, for whatever reason, imagined herself married to a clergyman.

Despite my attempt at confrontation, problems with her performance and behavior continued to occur. After hearing the report about the smell of alcohol on her breath, that became my frame of reference for dealing with her. Alcoholism I could understand. Personality disorder was not in my mental dictionary.

I encouraged her to seek treatment. She denied that she had a problem, made excuses, promised to go, and then backed out. Not wanting to repeat my predecessor's mistake, I didn't want to fire her. I wanted to get her help. I concluded that some form of intervention was necessary.

Eventually, I met with a small group of people off-site, including some of her best friends and some of the congregational leaders. I proposed to them that we confront her with her drinking problems and grant her a leave of absence to enter into a treatment program. I explained that if this was at all to succeed in getting her the help she needed, it was necessary that she not see any outs. We had to agree as a group that if she refused to go, her position would be terminated. They were hesitant but appeared to go along. They also agreed to secrecy so that she would not have an opportunity to find excuses or mount a defense before being presented with those alternatives. After our meeting, however, someone in the group shared the information with a family member, and the news quickly reached her. She was outraged and submitted her resignation even before I could talk with her. Predictably, much of the wrath of the congregation—when they found out about it—was directed at me.

Though the process was unpleasant, in some ways it was a good outcome for the congregation. We found a replacement, and almost overnight the continual upset and controversy that always seemed to surround the music program went away.

Shortly after that, I left the congregation to begin my training as a therapist. In one of my early days of training, as I was paging through the *Diagnostic and Statistical Manual of Mental Disorders*, Fourth Edition *(DSM-IV)*, the resource for psychologists and therapists in assigning diagnoses, I happened upon a description of borderline personality disorder. It described a person who exhibits: *"a pervasive pattern of instability of interpersonal relationships, self-image, and affects, and marked impulsivity."* It further indicated that he or she exhibits:

- *Frantic efforts to avoid real or imagined abandonment*
- *A pattern of unstable and intense interpersonal relationships characterized by alternating between extremes of idealization and devaluation*
- *Identity disturbance: markedly and persistently unstable self-image or sense of self*
- *Impulsivity in at less two areas that are potentially self-damaging (e.g., spending, sex, substance abuse, reckless driving, binge eating)*
- *Affective instability due to a marked reactivity of mood*
- *Chronic feelings of emptiness*
- *Inappropriate, intense anger or difficulty controlling anger*

I was astounded when I read that. I had no idea that there was a description of what I had been experiencing in my relationships with her, much less that there was actually a name for it. At seminary, I had taken a couple of courses on counseling, anticipating that it might be an important part of my ministry. I found them, however, to be rather unhelpful in providing practical techniques and skills that I could actually employ in a parish setting. At no point had I been introduced to personality disorders.

I suspect that more pastors today are at least familiar with the diagnosis of "borderline" than I was, as it is a diagnosis that has now entered more into common parlance, probably because of the notable turmoil these people create all around them. Still, the subject of personality disorders is one that, in general, appears not to be widely understood. Even less understood is any method for dealing with them when they occur in a parish situation, which most certainly, they will. According to statistical studies complied by the American Psychological Association, in a congregation of two hundred adults, if the congregation is at all representative of the general population as a whole, it most likely will have the following personality disorders in its church family: two paranoids, one schizoid, four schizotypals, two antisocials, two borderlines, four histrionics, two narcissists, two avoidants, four dependents, and eight obsessive compulsives. These are individuals who, in most circumstances, will appear quite "normal." They will not be crazy acting. They do not hear voices or act psychotic or need medication (medication, in fact, does not work with personality disorders). If you were to see them passing by, sitting in a church pew, or shaking hands with you at the door, in most cases, you would not notice anything distinctly unusual about them. Yet, they have a significant impairment in the way they relate to others. Thus, it is an impairment that often only becomes apparent in the kinds of interactions that congregations foster and encourage. These are not bad people or sick people. However, they are individuals who have a unique but also restricted way of dealing with the world: a way that sometimes keeps them isolated from others and sometimes creates intense havoc when they are involved. There is much that we now know about personality disorders—much of it only in recent times. *Reading this book will not qualify you to make personality disorder diagnoses. Official diagnosis should be left in the hands of mental health professionals who have the experience and ability to weigh all the factors that should go into a proper diagnosis.* However, growth in understanding personality types can broaden one's understanding of the way in which personality shapes the way an individual relates to the world. This knowledge can greatly enhance the way one relates to and manages challenging personalities in a community setting.

Knowledge of personality disorders is not the only psychological tool that is valuable for pastors to utilize. Family systems theory, which describes the dynamics of relationships, is an immensely beneficial concept that many pastors have found useful in understanding and working with the dynamics of their congregation. However, adding some knowledge of personality theory and the frames of references that different parties bring to a relationship can further enhance that understanding and provide additional tools for ministry.

This book will describe in some detail each of the ten personality disorders recognized by the American Psychological Association, providing also examples from congregational life. But first it is necessary to lay some groundwork. What exactly is a personality disorder and what creates it (Chapter 2)? How has the theory of understanding personalities evolved (Chapter 3)? What role do personality disorders play in congregational conflict (Chapter 4)? And, what is the theological understanding of relationships and what it means to be "in Christ" (Chapter 5)? The heart of this book then begins with Chapter 6, where you will be introduced to a general description of each of the personality disorders. The following ten chapters provide a more comprehensive description of each and snapshot examples of ways that these personalities have occurred in congregational life. Later chapters offer suggestions for providing both management and care for individuals with personality disorders as well as a chapter that looks at the personalities of congregational, and the dysfunctions they also sometimes exhibit.

2 WHAT IS A PERSONALITY DISORDER?

The *Diagnostic and Statistical Manual of Mental Disorders*, Fifth Edition (*DSM-5*), the current handbook for diagnostic criteria of the American Psychiatric Association, describes a personality disorder as: "an enduring pattern of inner experiences and behavior that deviates markedly from the expectations of the individual's culture."

This is a clinical description, useful in contexts where treatment is implied. I have some reservations about the use of the word *disorder* as applied to individuals in a congregational setting. It can certainly be misused to "*dis*" individuals: a way of labeling them as hopeless and problematic or, perversely, as a way to condone their behavior ("they can't help it"). Neither of those approaches would be helpful to the individuals involved or to the calling to care and minister. Congregations are not treatment centers. Jesus's instructions to Peter were to "feed my flock," not provide therapy for them. Yet a good shepherd, mindful of the flock, knows his or her sheep "by name." They are not all the same. They each have unique characteristics and idiosyncrasies that call for different kinds of care. Diagnosis is about "knowing." It is an aid to perceiving. Congregations are communities where individuals with a great variety of personality traits coexist. It is expedient for pastors and congregational leaders to be able to recognize and identify those whose patterns of behavior "deviate markedly" from expectations in order to provide appropriate management and care strategies that benefit both the individual and the congregation as a whole.

Disorder is a clinical term that indicates a degree of severity that leads to significant impairment of work or interpersonal functioning. It represents a point along a continuum where a certain personality trait stands out—"deviates markedly" from the norm. As you read the descriptions of the ten personality disorders, if you are like most, you will find that one or more of the descriptions will come close to describing you. That does not necessarily mean that you have the disorder. Only those that manifest most of the traits characteristic of that personality over a significant period of time and in a variety of circumstances are considered disorders. Those who only occasionally and in certain circumstances exhibit some of the traits are more aptly considered having a "personality style." In the later chapters that detail each of the ten personalities, general descriptions are given that further distinguish the differences between "disorder" and "style."

In any case, it should be understood here, that when the word *disorder* is used, it is used in a descriptive rather than a devaluating sense. To actually say to someone, "You have a personality disorder," would be extremely counterproductive; in part, because most likely you lack the experience and training to make such a judgment, but also because most likely the person addressed would experience that statement as a form of name-calling rather than as an expression of concern and care.

Knowing, however, the types of personality disorders can be quite useful for expanding one's ability to relate effectively with a wider variety of individuals. It is not unlike learning the names for different types of birds and animals.

My ability to identify birds used to be pretty limited. I could recognize robins, sparrows, blue jays, and cardinals (mostly because of their associations with sports teams), but that was about it. Anything else, if ever I noticed it, was simply "a bird." Then I got a backyard bird feeder. In addition to the above, I began to notice different kinds of birds: house finches and chickadees, nuthatches, and grosbeaks. And I began to notice different things about each kind of bird: some preferred different kinds of bird seed to others. Some only ate one seed at a time and would fly away to consume it (nuthatches). Others ate only on the ground (juncos). Others were picky (house finches), throwing the seeds that they didn't like on the ground (much to the delight of juncos). Some came only in pairs: if you saw a cardinal, you could be pretty certain that its mate was also somewhere nearby. Being able to name the birds was more than just an exercise in labeling. It enabled me to know how to attract different kinds of birds and the things to watch for when they came.

Likewise, being able to identify possible personality disorders is not really about labeling. God gave Adam the task of naming all of the animals because naming requires careful observation and identifying, a task that was an essential part of his responsibility to be a steward over "all the earth." A personality disorder does not make one a bad person, and the purpose of naming personality disorders is not to exclude certain types of people from congregations. Rather, it is a way of getting to know people more fully and to grow in awareness of the ways they can best fit into a congregational ministry. Recognizing how someone fits a certain behavioral type provides a measure of understanding. It is often a great relief to discover that there is a name for what one is experiencing, and it normalizes the experience. It also helps prevent an individual from being caught up in the dynamics that typically surround a personality disorder. Discovering that there is a name for the push and pull you have been experiencing in a relationship provides a context in which you can deepen your understanding of another and find helpful ways to respond. Personality disorders, as has already been hinted at, may be difficult to cure, but they can be managed. Sheep are free-range animals and are typically not fenced, but the hook on the shepherd's staff was designed to establish boundaries when needed. Understanding personality disorders provides you with a new pair of eyes and a new tool kit for responding effectively to the different kinds of people you encounter in parish ministry. The ultimate purpose of this book is to serve as a shepherd's guide for minding the flock.

Personalities

Personality, defined psychologically, is the set of enduring behavioral and mental traits that distinguish human beings.

Human beings are distinguished by appearance: height, eye and hair color, the shape of one's chin, eyelash length, dimples, etc. These are traits inherited through genetic transmission. Inherited traits, however, include not only the way one looks but also the way one tends to think, feel, and act. Whether or not one is adventurous, cautious, determined, outgoing, shy, or optimistic, also appears to be largely inherited. Together, these traits make up one's personality. Personality is like the brain's operating system. Certain neural highways are the preferred pathways along which information and response flow.

Personality is "enduring"—not easy to change. It can be adapted, but only with effort and over a period of time. For example, some who enter ministry are by nature introverts. Because their calling demands that they be sociable and outgoing, many are able to develop those roles and behaviors when called upon to do so, but to some extent, this is always energy draining because it requires effort. To a similar degree, personality *disorders* are also resistant to change, not only because they are *enduring*, but also because they appear to offer fewer choices for adaptability. Thus, one of the features of a disordered personality is its lack of flexibility. A personality is like a tool kit from which one can draw out different tools to utilize in different roles that we assume in life. We might talk and act one way with our closest friends but quite differently with members of our congregation. But an individual with a personality disorder has a limited number of tools in his or her kit. Some of the tools might work and function quite properly in some of their roles and settings but entirely inappropriately in others. A narcissistic pastor might serve quite ably as a fundraiser for his or her congregation but be totally inept at dealing with staff or with members of his or her family. A disordered personality has more difficulty than most in being able to make the changes necessary to function appropriately in different circumstances and conditions. This lack of flexibility and adaptability is one of the key markers of a disorder. In an age of growing complexity that requires greater flexibility, personality disorders are becoming more evident.

Often, individuals with personality disorders are not even aware of how their own personalities might be contributing to the way others react and respond. They lack the ability to see themselves accurately. Psychologists call it a lack of an observing ego. Unlike other mental health conditions, such as depression or anxiety or post-traumatic stress disorder, personality disorders do not normally go away after a period of time. Generally, medications are ineffective, and there are no known medications for the treatment of specific personality disorders. Data from a longitudinal study of individuals who have been diagnosed with a personality disorder show that, though some change occurred, the rate of change was very low compared to treatments for other mental health issues.

Personality disorders are often underdiagnosed or unrecognized because they can present with vague, general, indistinct, and even benign-sounding (although chronic) complaints. Typically, if individuals are experiencing difficulties, they see others as the cause of those difficulties and thus are not apt to seek counseling or even advice. They often are at risk for other serious life and medical problems. Many times they experience marriage difficulties, and because the nature of the personality disorder is not recognized, traditional marriage counseling often fails. They often have frequent physical complaints. Certain personality disorders are at high risk for sexual misconduct or for substance abuse.

The *DSM-5*'s description that personality disorders "deviate markedly from the expectations of the individual's culture" is noteworthy. It implies that in many areas of life, such an individual may function quite normally. It is only when it comes up against certain "expectations" that difficulty arises. These expectations, the *DSM* tactfully suggests, are not universally normative but are culturally determined. Thus, these expectations may differ from group to group. For example, an individual with obsessive compulsive disorder might function quite well in a job as a mechanical engineer, where a high degree of accuracy and perfectionism is required, but might experience considerable turmoil in a marriage where this individual's efforts at control create constant turmoil.

Congregations are often notable for their low degree of expectations. "All are welcome," is a frequently used promotional refrain. As a result, individuals with personality disorder at first aren't always noticed. Some congregations proceed many years without significant problems, only to be surprised when suddenly there is a great deal of conflict. Typically, the conflict arises when some event—the need to make a decision about a sexuality statement or the decision about whether or not to relocate or to merge with another congregation—suddenly raises the level of expectations, and what was long hidden suddenly emerges full blown. And in other situations, though the behavior is certainly noticed and visible, it has become normative. It is the way people are. Like some marriages that appear to thrive on constant arguments and bickering, some congregations have come to accept the unusual behavior of some of their members and are reluctant to consider the possibility that there might be different ways as a community to manage such behavior.

The Cause of Personality Disorder

So, are personalities and personality disorders a result of genetics or of environmental experiences?

In 1943, as some of the fiercest fighting of World War II took place, Abraham Maslow published an article titled "A Theory of Human Motivation." He intended, in part, to try to understand what it was that drove people to follow monomaniacal leaders such as Hitler and Stalin. But he also wanted to understand as much as possible what made a person "normal"—capable of being happy, productive, pleasant, and able to enjoy intellectual and aesthetic pursuits. This was a new twist for psychology, which for the most part up until then had focused on the abnormal: the behaviors and mood disorders that led to severe dysfunction. Maslow also wanted to make room for "unmotivated behavior," the playfulness and aesthetic enjoyment that often appear spontaneously among humans. Freud had sought to identify the "drives," the forces operating both consciously and subconsciously that shape human behavior. Maslow recognized that in certain respects, human behavior is indeed internally driven—that motivation often comes as a result of unfulfilled needs. But he also wanted to describe the conditions under which motivation is not driven but freely chosen.

Maslow concluded that there were indeed certain basic needs among people of all cultures that often create powerful motivational forces. As he studied their lives and their motivations, he developed a theory of a "hierarchy of needs." Certain basic needs, he argued, predominate until they are sufficiently met, and only then do additional needs come to the fore. "It is true," he observed, "that man does not live by bread alone. But what happens to man's desires," he continued, "when there is plenty of bread?" As basic and foundational needs are met, other and higher needs emerge.

He created a pyramid to depict the ascending needs through which a child develops. At the base of the pyramid, he placed physiological needs: primarily the need for food and touch. Failure to meet these basic physiological needs results in adults with low frustration tolerance, high tension, and little stamina.

The next step on Maslow's pyramid is the need for safety. Children require a sense of security. They like repetition, which assures them that the world is reliable. Failure to meet the needs of safety results in adults who feel insecure and exhibit obsession and compulsion tendencies.

The third step of the pyramid represents the need for love. Children need to experience unconditional love: to know that even though they sometimes make mistakes or fail does not destroy the bond of love. Failure results in adults who have deep seated feelings of worthlessness, emptiness, and incompleteness.

The fourth step is the need for esteem—to be recognized and applauded for one's gifts and achievements. Failure results in adults with a feeling of inferiority and a sense of incompetence.

The apex of Maslow's pyramid represents the need for self-actualization, the experience that one has the power to choose. Failure results in adults who live by routine, who feel alienated from the world, and who fear that their life has no meaning.

Drawing on the work of Maslow, Gary McIntosh, a professor of Christian ministry and leadership at Talbot School of Theology, joined with Samuel Rina, Sr, a faculty member in the Center for Transformational Leadership at Bethel Seminary in St. Paul, Minnesota, to produce a book titled *Overcoming the Dark Side of Leadership*. Though they don't directly reference the *DSM*, their description of five types of "dark-side leadership" appear to be taken directly from personality disorders described in the *DSM-III*: the compulsive leader, the narcissistic leader, the paranoid leader, the codependent leader, and the compulsive leader. They argue that these personality types develop in early childhood and are a way of coping when a basic need is not fully met. Their basic schema is this: every child has certain basic needs that must be met in order to mature fully. Due to trauma or neglect, some of those needs are not adequately met, leading to an existential and emotional emptiness. This feeling of a personal failing often leads to adults being driven to try to fulfill those needs, often acting in childish and immature ways. Personality disorders, from this point of view, are the attempts to pay off this emotional debt through unhealthy behaviors in the adult years.

Thus, according to McIntosh and Rima, all of us to some degree have a "dark side," as none of us have had a perfect childhood. And, to the degree that certain basic needs have been unmet, we have within us basic drives that will act out inappropriately in certain circumstances unless we become more aware of these tendencies and understand the reason for them. This was the exposition of that "other law" that the Apostle Paul described in Romans 7, which wages "war against the law of my mind and making me a prisoner of the law of sin at work within my members" (v. 23).

It is a description that appeals in its simplicity and can be quite helpful for many people. The only problem is, it isn't entirely accurate.

Similar to McIntosh and Rima, therapists for many years have believed that disruption to early childhood attachment led to the establishment of a personality structure that produced distorted experience and dysfunctional behavior. This seemed to be consistent with their experience, as nearly all people in treatment for personality disorder had experienced sexual abuse as a child or had hypercritical or absent parents. The only problem with this understanding was that it was entirely anecdotal and theory based, with little data-based analysis. It didn't explain, for example, why 80 percent of those with a history of sexual abuse *do not* develop a personality disorder.

More recently, it has been argued that personality disorders are genetically transmitted. Studies were conducted on both identical and fraternal twins. It was established that among identical twins, similarity of personality hovered around 46 percent, while for fraternal twins, personality similarities were 23 percent. This seemed to establish that there was at least a substantial genetic link to personality. This would account for the relative stability of personality disorders as well as for their early appearance—in some cases, the features of a personality disorder can already be discerned in a child between the ages of three to five. It would also explain the difficulty of traditional "talk therapy" in providing treatment.

It might also explain one of the essential features of personality disorders: the relative lack of self-awareness. Those with personality disorders often seem totally oblivious to the effects their behavior has on those around them and have little understanding of how their own behavior and conduct may have contributed to it. This may relate to a genetic disturbance of the "mirror neurons" of the brain.

In the 1980s and 1990s, a group of neurophysiologists at the University of Parma in Italy were conducting research on macaque monkeys to study the neurons specialized for the control of hand and mouth movements. By placing an electrode in the brain, they were able to monitor the actions of individual neurons as the monkey took hold of a piece of food and manipulated it. They were surprised to discover that some neurons responded when the monkey observed another person pick up the food as well as when the monkey itself did. They called these neurons "mirror neurons." They wrote up their discovery and sent it to the science magazine *Nature* for publication, but as often happens to new discoveries, it was rejected due to its "lack of general interest." Later, when mirror neurons were also located in the human brain, the material received a great deal of interest. It is now believed that mirror neurons largely contribute to humans' ability to experience empathy, and, though this is still an item for further research, an impairment of these mirror neurons may also contribute to personality disorders.

Still, the studies indicated that something less than half of personality is genetically determined. Attempts to link specific kinds of personalities with specific genes have so far failed.

The current theories about the cause of personality disorders is called "biopsychosocial"—that genetic temperament facts (heredity and neurology) combine with psychological, environmental, and social experiences to create a pattern of distorted experience and dysfunctional behavior.

That may sound a lot like, "We really don't know what creates personalities and personality disorders," which is partially true. Personalities are a complex mix of many factors. Humans don't come preassembled. The basic pieces are glued together by life because both genetics and experience affect the neuronal connections in the brain—the way we are "wired." We don't fully choose our identity nor do we need to be fully bound by the current structure of it. God may indeed create "my inmost being" and "knit me together in my mother's womb" (Psalm 139:13), but he also discerns "my going out and my lying down" and is "familiar with all my ways" (Ps. 139:3). All of this together creates the unique human beings that we are.

3 DEFINING PERSONALITIES: FOUR HUMORS AND FIVE DSMS

The idea that certain personality types are "disorders" is a relatively recent idea, dating, as we shall see, from 1980. In fact, the word "personality" itself as a description of "a distinctive character" was first used only in 1795.

Thus, it is not surprising that a word for "personality" is not found in the biblical literature, though certain personality characteristics are recognizable in many of the people described in the Bible: the differences between Jacob and Esau, Peter's extroversion (always the first to speak up, Mt. 16:15-16), Thomas's pessimism ("Let us also go that we may die with him," John 11:16), Saul's initial shyness (hiding in the baggage when Samuel came to anoint him king, I Sam. 10:24). The only word that even comes close to what we mean by personality is the word Χαρακτηρ (character), a word used only once (Heb. 1:3). The word means "engraved image," and its use in Hebrews describes Jesus: "The Son is the radiance of God's glory and the *exact representation* of his being."

Scripture assigns all human "disorders" to one category: sin. There may be many different words for sin—*falling short, disobedience, trespass, iniquity, impurity*. There also may be many descriptors of the variety of forms sin can take, such as Paul's list of the works of the flesh in Galatians 5—"sexual immorality, impurity and debauchery; idolatry and witchcraft; hatred, discord, jealousy, fits of rage, selfish ambition, dissensions, factions, and envy; drunkenness, orgies, and the like"—but these are arguably descriptions of behavior, not of character or personality. If one were to attempt to describe "personality" from a purely Scriptural perspective, there would be only one option: the disorder that theologians describe as "original sin." This concept makes it clear that human disorder has less to do with specific actions or failures of action that result in guilt, but that it lies much deeper in the condition of humanity itself and the consequent experience of shame. Something is deficient in the personality of all. Due to this deeper underlying condition, the attempts at self-reformation and self-help always end in failure. As Paul so notably described: "For I have the desire to do what is good, but I cannot carry it out. For what I do is not the good I want to do; no the evil I do not want to do—this I keep on doing. Now, if I do what I do not want to do, it is no longer I who do it, but it is sin living in me that does it. So I find this law at work: When I want to do good, evil is right there with me. For in my inner being I delight in God's law; but I see another law at work in the members of my body, waging war against the law of my mind and making me a prisoner of the law of sin at work within my members" (Rom 7:18b-23).

The result of all humanity falling into one category is clear: "All have sinned and fall short of the glory of God" (Rom 3:23). A discussion of personality disorders does not change that biblical truth. In terms of achieving righteousness before God, there are not some personalities better than others. Likewise, in terms of being hopeless, outside the realm of God's grace and love, no personality type is excluded.

So, if Scripture makes a point of not distinguishing between persons, what is the usefulness of delineating different types of personality disorders? Though there is a tendency in Christian circles to want to "baptize" psychological theory before accepting it, claiming it merely demonstrates and further elucidates ancient biblical principles, there is no real need. Personality theory is a way of looking at human behavior, which for the most part is a very recent development. Biblical writers neither accepted it nor rejected it, because it was not at all within their frame of reference. That it is outside of biblical perspective does not mean that it cannot be knowledge that is useful to know. The technology of computers and sound systems are also outside of a biblical frame of reference but have often proven to be quite useful for congregations. Likewise, especially when it comes to understanding the dynamics of congregations, knowledge of personality disorders can be quite beneficial.

Theophrastus

The earliest attempt to categorize different types of individuals into groups, as far as we know, was undertaken by Theophrastus (371 to 287 BC), a favorite disciple of Aristotle, who, before his death, Aristotle made both guardian of his children and his designated successor at the Lyceum. Theophrastus (a nickname given to him by Aristotle, meaning something like "divine speaker") is perhaps best known for his study of plants and is considered the "father of botany." Applying the same procedures he applied to the classification of plants, he categorized different personality types in a brief work titled *Characters (Χαρακτηρες—i.e.,* the same root word as that used to describe Jesus's indelible character in Hebrews). His prologue begins, "I have often marveled, when I have given the matter my attention, and it may be I shall never cease to marvel, why it has come about that, albeit the whole of Greece lies in the same clime and all Greeks have a like upbringing, we have not the same constitution of character." *(The Characters of Theophrastus,* edited by J. M. Edmonds, New York: G. P. Putnam & Sons, 1929) In what follows, he does not pursue the "why" question, but instead he provides descriptive details of thirty different "constitutions of character": dissembler, flatterer, garrulous, boor, self-seeker, reckless, loquacious, gossip, shameless, miser, buffoon, tactless, officious, stupid, rude, superstitious, grumbler, distrustful, nasty, annoying, pettily proud, parsimonious, pretentious, arrogant, cowardly, domineering, slow learner, backbiter, friend of rascals, and mean.

A quick survey of the list reveals that what Theophrastus is describing would not normally be described as vices, but patterns of behavior deficient in meeting social norms. His use of the word Χαρακτηρ to delineate them indicates that these patterns have a certain indelible quality that persists through time. At least some of his descriptors would be capable of traveling through time to find their place in a modern description of personality disorder: "The...man of a kind that when he is invited out to dine must needs to find a place to dine next to the host" ("pettily proud": narcissistic). "When he is abed he will ask his wife if the coffer be locked and the cupboard sealed and the house-door bolted, and for all she may say Yes, he will himself rise naked and bare-foot from the blankets and light the candle and run round the house to see" ("distrustful": obsessive-compulsive).

Theophrastus wrote at a time when the Old Testament Canon was complete; therefore, one does not expect to find any resonance with his ideas there. But there are also no indications that any of the New Testament writers were aware of his work or were influenced by his ideas in how they thought about people. Though the Apostle Paul was knowledgeable of many of the writings of the classical Greeks and could quote them to the philosophers in the Areopagus, none of his list of fifteen "works of the flesh" in Galatians 5 correspond to any of Theophrastus's list, indicating that he had something entirely different in mind.

The Four Humors Theory

Though Theophrastus provides an interesting insight into an early attempt to describe different character types, it did not, as far as can be discerned, have widespread influence. That is not the case with the four humors theory first proposed by the Greek physician Hippocrates (460-370 BC), a theory that became the definitive description of personality for nearly twenty centuries. Since the body, according to the ancient understanding of human anatomy, is filled with four types of fluids, the purpose of which was not always known, it made sense to Hippocrates to suggest that they might have different causative factors. He proposed that certain human moods, emotions, and behaviors were the result of an imbalance of these fluids: blood, yellow bile (believed to be secreted by the liver), black bile (believed to be secreted by the kidneys or spleen), and phlegm.

Galen, who lived shortly after the New Testament period (AD 131–200) is credited with taking this simple idea and developing the first typology of temperament in his dissertation *De temperamentis*. Like Hippocrates, he believed that there were physiological reasons for different behaviors in humans. He connected Hippocrates's four humors with what were then believed to be the four basic elements of all matter—earth, air, fire, and water—and devised a scheme for identifying four basic types of temperaments: melancholic (an excess of black bile, earth), phlegmatic (an excess of phlegm, water), sanguine (an excess of blood, air), and choleric (an excess of yellow bile, fire). Because this typology was widely known, people often would identify themselves as one of these. Martin Luther, for example, considered himself choleric, answering one of his critics: "I own that I am more vehement than I ought to be; but I have to do with men who blaspheme evangelical truth; with human wolves; with those who condemn me unheard, without admonishing, without instructing me; and who utter the most atrocious slanders against myself not only, but the Word of God. Even the most *phlegmatic* spirit, so circumstanced, might well be moved to speak thunderbolts; much more I who am *choleric* by nature, and possessed of a temper easily apt to exceed the bounds of moderation."

These classifications provided a guide to treatment, as physicians utilized a variety of methods, including bloodletting, hot baths, medicated steam, chest poultices, gargles, and laxatives to add to or subtract from the fluids in the body to achieve a balance.

Personality Disorders and Psychoanalytic Theory

Only toward the later part of the nineteenth century and the scientific revolution, with its emphasis upon empiricism and classification, did the theory of the four humors as the source of differences between people finally begin to crumble. Careful observation led to the conclusion that it was not bodily fluids but the work of the body's neurological system that controlled human behavior. The word "pscyhosis," meaning literally a "disorder of the soul" was first used in 1841 by Karl Friedrich Canstatt in his *Handbuch der Medizinischen Klinik*. He used it to describe what he considered to be the manifestation of brain disease.

Initial efforts at determining how the neurological system functioned were focused upon neurological extremes—i.e., mental disorders. Emil Kraepeling (1856-1926), a German psychologist, furthered the work on mental disorders through careful classification into categories according to symptoms. He maintained that psychiatry was a branch of medical science, which, like other natural sciences, should proceed by careful observation and experimentation. He proposed that by studying case histories, it would be possible to identify specific disorders that could lead to the ability to predict the progression of the illness.

And then came Sigmund Freud (1856-1939). As a scientist wanting to describe cause and effect, but lacking the instrumentation to actually examine how neurons worked, he theorized various forces that worked subliminally, naming them "id," "ego," and "superego." His theory, for the first time, provided a method of treatment for the mentally ill. Instead of being locked up in insane asylums, they could be treated through psychoanalysis: where the client reclining on a couch simply talked in free-form fashion, while the clinician, whose task it was to "analyze" watched for details that could explain the forces at work.

Because at the time there were no significant competing theories or treatments, his ideas became widely known and established. Today, more significant means of determining neurological functioning are now available, and different forms of treatment, based upon clinical studies of results, are now available. Many of Freud's hypotheses are no longer accepted, but his influenced continued well into the twentieth century and into the first attempts to formally classify mental disorders.

The Diagnostic and Statistical Manuals and Personality Disorder Descriptions

Many psychiatrists became involved with selection, assessment, and treatment of soldiers during World War II. In an effort to standardize classification and treatment, a new classification scheme called Medical 203 was devised by Dr. Menninger during the war. In 1952, under the auspices of the American Psychological Association, this became the basis for the first *Diagnostic and Statistical Manual of Mental Disorders* (*DSM*), a guide still in use today (now in its current edition, the *DSM-5*) as the definitive resource for diagnosis by therapists, psychologists, and psychiatrists. The first edition was heavily influenced by Freudian theory and adopted many of his terms. As the efforts to this point had primarily been the diagnosis and treatment of psychosis, no distinctions involving personality problems were included, though "personality disturbances" were sometimes included with other disorders.

The first revision of the *DSM* (*DSM-II*) occurred in 1968. The Freudian influence continued and the diagnostic system was almost exclusively psychoanalytically based. Personality problems were viewed primarily as developmental issues that could lead to various psychiatric conditions.

By the 1970s, many were beginning to realize that psychiatry had arrived at a dead end. Psychoanalysis was by and large not producing results. The American Psychological Association put Dr. Robert Spitzer in charge of developing a new edition of the *DSM*. He proposed doing away with theory-based descriptions (i.e., psychoanalytic theory) and instead utilized experimental, reliable, scientific methods and descriptions to describe psychiatric conditions. The result was the discovery or highlighting of what many clinicians had claimed: that there were patients who didn't fit the criteria for psychiatric disorders but who still were significantly impaired or distressed. These were individuals who appeared to have good reality testing but continued to have some form of continuing low-grade distress in their lives. They did not seem to respond to treatment. They could frequently be demanding, unreasonable, or unpleasant and often produced confusion and upset those around them.

Thus, when this new edition of the *DSM* came out in 1980 (*DSM-III*), for the first time there was a separate category for these "nonfitting" patients. It drew a distinction between "illness" and "disorder." Conditions like depression, anxiety, post-traumatic stress, like an illness, could be described as having "symptoms" and followed a certain "progression," but "disorders," by contrast, had "characteristics" and were "pervasive" and "enduring." Thus, the *DSM-III* proposed a multiaxial system for diagnosis to acknowledge the complexity of forces that impacted a person's functioning. Axis I was the category for traditional psychiatric disorders. Axis III looked at medical conditions, recognizing that often those issues could affect functioning. Axis IV looked at environmental factors, such as living conditions, employment, family status, etc. Axis V was a way of designating severity. Axis II, however, for the first time, was an attempt to look at personality disorders, acknowledging that they could both coexist with psychiatric problems (Axis I) or in some cases occur without psychiatric disorders. Eleven personality disorders were defined in this edition of the *DSM*, grouped into three different categories: odd, dramatic, and anxious. A revision was made in 1987 (*DSM-III-R*) that added two additional personality disorders and established a threshold for diagnosis (i.e., an individual needed to meet a certain number of the criteria that described that disorder).

With the *DSM-IV*, first published in 1994, the number of personality disorders, based upon further research, was established as ten. They were: paranoid, schizoid, schizotypal, antisocial, borderline, histrionic, narcissistic, avoidant, dependent, and obsessive-compulsive. These are the ten personality styles and disorders that we will be examining in closer detail in chapters seven to sixteen.

A new edition of the *DSM* (*DSM-5*) was published in 2013. In this edition, the multiaxial system was dropped, but the ten personality disorders were retained and listed alongside the other diagnoses of mental illness.

Wayne Oates and *Behind the Masks*

The word *workaholic* was first coined by Wayne Oates. As it is often said, "it takes one to know one." The author of fifty-seven books—in addition to his active career as a religious educator who was largely responsible for shaping the modern pastoral care movement, was seldom idle. At the age of fifty-seven, he joined the department of psychiatry and behavioral sciences of the University of Louisville School of Medicine and worked there for the next eighteen years, frequently participating in case conferences and grand rounds with members of the staff.

Partly as a result of his experiences there, in 1987 he published the first book about personality disorders, intended for religious professionals. He titled it *Behind the Masks: Personality Disorders in Religious Behavior*. In choosing that title, he admitted to drawing heavily upon a book written by Hervey Cleckley titled *The Mask of Sanity*. Cleckley described how certain psychopathic persons frequently could mimic a normally functioning person, able to mask or disguise the lack of a stable internal personality structure, which often resulted in destructive behavior directed at others or oneself. He observed that often these people, while seemingly sincere, intelligent, or even charming, did not appear to have the ability to experience genuine emotions. He wasn't sure whether this "mask of sanity" was deliberately assumed in order to hide what was recognized as internal shortcomings from others, or if the mask was simply a result of a serious psychiatric defect.

Wayne Oates indicated that he wrote the book because he believed that: "the goal of church leaders and mentors is to 'unmask' these behaviors so that the 'image of God' could be seen instead." At the same time, he indicated that his purpose was "to 'defuse name-calling' that 'downgrades' Christian brothers and sisters." Much of what he wrote is still of value today. Still, more than twenty-five years have passed since then, during which time the understanding of personality disorders has been further refined and clarified. His descriptions were based on only seven (including "passive-aggressive," which is no longer recognized as a separate disorder) of the eleven disorders listed in the *DSM-III,* **the edition that was available to him**. Likewise, some would find his attempt to draw guidelines for each disorder from the Old Testament wisdom literature as well as from the parables of Jesus a bit of a stretch. Meanwhile, the need to have some means of understanding these disorders and guidelines for working with them, particularly as they apply to the working of voluntary communities of people such as congregations, is even more urgent now as the tensions in congregations with dwindling numbers has increased exponentially since the 1980s.

We live at a time when advances in technology have made remarkable improvements in communication possible. Virtually instant and individual communication, often accompanied by visual images and sound, is now possible to almost any place in the world. Many congregations have availed themselves of these new technologies, using media in their worship services and communicating with their membership through websites, Twitter feeds, Facebook, electronic newsletters, and other means. But while means of transmitting content has improved dramatically, almost no progress has been made in communicating and understanding the emotions that go along with the content. The emotional content of communication is the essential ingredient of relationships, and until gains are made in recognizing and responding appropriately to such content, all the technological improvements will help little to improve the functioning of congregations.

4 CONGREGATIONS AND CONFLICT

The English language has the curious distinction of utilizing different words for gatherings of different animals. A group of geese is a flock; a group of wolves, a pack; a group of sheep, a flock; a group of ants, a colony; a group of crows, a murder; and a group of alligators, a congregation. The latter is likely the derivation for the relatively common use among clergy of the term "alligators" to describe difficult or critical parishioners. For some in parish ministry, it does seem at times as if the parish has become a swamp infested with dangerous critters.

In 1998, Ken Haugk, a pastor and clinical psychologist and the founder of the Stephen Series, a system of training lay people for caring ministry, produced a book titled *Antagonists in the Church.* It acknowledged, perhaps for the first time in print, that many congregations had become battlegrounds. Disagreements were often escalating into outright conflict, where opponents were vilified, whisper campaigns organized, rumors spread, and confrontations occurred that sometimes escalated to shouting and even physical violence. Haugk's book singled out the presence of "antagonists" in congregations. He defined them broadly as having "five personality characteristics": negative self-concept, narcissism, aggression, rigidity, and authoritarianism. He acknowledged that some of these personality traits may also occur in "normal" individuals, but that antagonists typically exhibit more than one of the five characteristics and also have extreme forms of them.

A few years later, G. Lloyd Redinger upped the ante by producing a book titled *Clergy Killers: Guidance for Pastors and Congregations under Attack.* He contended that often what was occurring in congregations was more than mere differences of principled opinions, personality conflicts, or poor communication. Rather, the conflict involved persistent and deliberate attacks. Though he does mention that sometimes the role is reversed and clergy can be destructive of congregations, the use of the provocative word *killers* in the title and his encouragement to view antagonists as "evil," requiring some form of exorcism, raised the issue of problem parishioners to new levels. The book became a best seller among his intended audience and was widely read and quoted, indicating that he was addressing a problem that many had experienced.

Statistics about clergy leaving parish ministry would seem to bear that out.

In 1999, the Lutheran Church—Missouri Synod—commissioned Alan C. Klaas and Cheryl D. Klaas to conduct a study that would address the possibility of a looming clergy shortage. The assumption at the beginning of the survey was that the problem chiefly related to an insufficient number of candidates entering seminary. The study found, however, that the heart of the problem lay elsewhere. More pastors were leaving parish ministry each year than were removed from the roll due to retirement or death, a surprising finding since it is widely assumed that ministry is a lifetime vocation. The study included numerous focus groups that found a high degree of burnout among 20 percent of those surveyed.

Statistics from other denominations are uneven, each looking at different parameters, but the overall conclusion is the same: ministry has become a high-stress occupation that many are leaving, sometimes voluntarily, sometimes by forced resignations. A United Methodist study found that 41 percent of their clergy left in the first ten years of ministry. A 1988 ELCA study found that 15 percent resigned or were removed from the roster during their first thirteen years of ministry. A 1998 Presbyterian study estimated that between 11 and 13 percent ordained between 1990-1992 had already left the ministry. A study done by the *Francis A. Schaeffer Institute of Church Leadership Development* among evangelical pastors concluded that between 35 percent and 40 percent of pastors will ultimately leave ministry, most within the first five years. A Roman Catholic survey conducted in 2001 found that between 10 and 12 percent of priests leave within the first five years.

Some of these studies also included interviews with those who have left. A variety of reasons were offered, including: lack of congregational support, unrealistic expectations and demands of parishioners, lack of denominational support, and no shared vision. But a common theme running through most of the interviews was the issue of conflict: conflict with parishioners, with other staff members, or with denominational officials.

In many cases, "leaving ministry," it should be noted, does not equate with losing faith or even with giving up on the institution of the church. Many of those no longer serving in parish ministry continue to serve in some other form of church work, including chaplaincy, teaching at religious institutions, and serving in parachurch organizations. In these cases, the issues seem to be not so much faith or doctrinal issues as the practical difficulties of working in parish ministry.

It is not hard to see that the statistics on pastors leaving ministry roughly parallels what is taking place on the other side of the pulpit: the general decline in congregational membership.

The Pew Research Center's Forum on Religion & Public Life, which has conducted intensive surveys on the nature of religion in America, coined a new word to describe a significant finding—the "nones," those who say they have no religious affiliation. The number of Americans who do not identify with any religion continues to grow at a rapid pace and now outnumbers any particular denomination. They found that in the '90s, the percentage of "nones" doubled from 7 percent to 14 percent of the US population. And the numbers have continued to rise. The 2012 survey recorded that the "nones" now account for one-fifth of the US public. Among adults under thirty, the number is one in three.

The Nashville-based Glenmary Research Center has conducted a survey of religious membership in America once every ten years since 1970. Their surveys indicate that while the actual number of members in religious congregations has continued to grow, the overall percentage in comparison to the US population has declined somewhat. In 1980, the total number of members stood at 112 million (50 percent of the population). In 2010, the number was 150 million (48.8 percent of the population).

The Gallup research found that in 2010, 77 percent of the population still identified themselves as "Christian." Yet their surveys also indicated that between 1978 and 2001, the percent of the US population that was unchurched grew from 41 percent to 47 percent.

Statistics here can become slippery, as you will note that the numbers don't always seem to be consistent. Part of the reason for this is different survey parameters, such as the years analyzed or the definitions used. There is, for example, a difference between those who, when asked, will claim membership in a particular denomination, even though they are not found on any church roll; those who are nominally members of a particular congregation but who seldom if ever attend; and those who are active members in congregations, participating regularly. Congregations and denominations also have different ways of counting membership. There are also conflicting trends: some congregations are growing rapidly, while others are growing slowly or, in some cases, swiftly dying. Likewise, some religious denominations are seeing growth, while others have experienced years of decline. And some are growing, but their pace of growth falls behind the general population growth. However, I believe that few who have been involved in some way in congregations over the past twenty to thirty years would disagree that congregations face stiffer challenges now than ever before in attracting and retaining membership.

This book is about personality disorders, and one might expect the argument to be made that the failure to recognize and respond effectively to these individuals is a prime reason for the deline in church membership. However, the factors that lead to abandonment of active participation in a faith community and the trajectories of those departures are many and diverse. Congregational conflict resulting from the difficulty of working with personality disorders is one, but there are many others as well. Some drift away for no apparent reason. For others, however, a hurtful encounter is the impetus for leaving church: the failure to be supported in a time of need, an experience of being criticized or judged by pastors or members, or simply discouragement over the intensity of arguments and feuds that arise in a congregation over seemingly minor issues. For others, it is the incongruence between what is said and what is practiced. For still others, abandoning church is not due to any particularly bad experience but rather to the gradual realization that participation in worship services hadn't led to a deepened experience of God.

Some would argue that the decline of active participation in congregations merely follows wider trends occurring in society. Community organizations of all types—from PTAs to Kiwanis clubs to bowling leagues—have experienced loss of membership, as sociologist Robert Putnam demonstrated in his book *Bowling Alone*. Multigenerational families are scattered geographically. Individuals move, and change jobs frequently. Front porches, which allowed for social networking in neighborhoods, have given way to houses fronted by two- and three-car garages. The social institutions that used to provide the opportunity and the place for developing significant relationships are in decline.

Others would argue that congregations have lost one of their core sociological functions: fostering cultural identity. Several generations ago, newly arriving immigrants quickly founded churches that helped foster ethnic and social values from the old country. Germans, Swedes, Danes, Italians, and others joined congregations of like-minded individuals. The social and cultural heritage created ties that worked for several generations to bind families to congregations. However, as individuals became more assimilated to American culture, this binding force lessened. One can see the same force at work in newly arriving immigrant groups, such as Hispanics (a significant factor in maintaining the numbers of Roman Catholics), Sudanese, Karen, Bhutanese, and other ethnic groups arriving as refugees on American shores.

News and media images of clergy and congregations also have played a role. Compared to the 1950s and 1960s, where religion was often portrayed in a positive light (e.g., *A Man Called Peter, The Ten Commandments, The Shoes of the Fisherman*) and religion was occasionally a popular subject for *Saturday Evening Post* covers, news media, books, and movies, now, more often than not, portray churchgoers and believers as judgmental, hypocritical, dim-witted, and narrow-minded. In the movie *Oh, God!*, George Burns, playing the role of God, attempts to recruit a reluctant Jerry Landers to be his spokesman. At one point, Jerry objects: "But I don't even go to church," to which God replies, "Neither do I."

While churchgoing and religion in general are often rejected, an interest in spirituality continues to be maintained. A significant feature of spirituality is its individualism. You can practice it, foster it, and experience it any way you want. It doesn't require convincing or being convinced by someone else that yours is the true path. It is by definition incapable of being judged. Others may criticize it, which is their right or perhaps their ignorance, but spirituality doesn't require getting along with others.

Then, there is simply the matter of busyness. Busyness has become a way of life, and in a schedule already overcrowded with work requirements, social events, and children's school and sport activities, church participation often appears to be expendable.

The rise of social media may also be playing a role. Electronic social networking sites provide alternatives and often result in a broader and far more active network of connections. But there is a different nature to these connections. They appear to provide a kind of pseudocommunity. It can, on the one hand, be quite self-affirming to know that someone in cyberspace responds because I just typed, "Am sitting on my deck feeling bored." The frequency and immediacy of these interchanges can become quite addictive, causing one to check Facebook sites and Twitter accounts throughout the day and to become anxious, almost panicky, when access is lost. Yet, these are relationships that often lack the authenticity, duration, and commitment needed for deepened relationships—the kind that are capable of bridging differences and weathering storms. If there is a theme to this, it would seem to be that there are far more opportunities today to create and maintain relationships with those with whom a common interest is shared but a disinclination to invest the time, effort, and discomfort to work through relationships that may have become problematic (i.e., those required to continue an active participation in congregational life).

Most of this is not new to any who work with

congregations. These factors cumulatively create a situation where tensions run high. Many congregations operate with a survival mentality. Fear takes hold. Expectations are high; hope is low. Minor failings or shortcomings seem magnified. Blame becomes easier than praise. The result is often conflict. People do not join congregations or participate in congregations in order to argue and fight. Most often, they are seeking comfort, peace, friendship, acceptance, and guidance. Conflicts often result in polarization, where both sides become highly invested in their positions. But there is also often another group who couldn't care less. And in the face of unpleasant experiences, these are the ones who simply drift away.

More often than not, the presence of personality disorders, sometimes in the person of the pastor and sometimes in that of lay leaders, is a significant factor that contributes to a failure to arrive at solutions when disagreements occur. When I first began working on this book, I contacted a number of pastors with whom I was acquainted to see if they knew of examples of any of the ten personality disorders. "You mean there are only ten?" one replied.

There may be good reason to believe that personality disorders are present in congregations perhaps to an even greater degree than in the population in general:

1) Congregations seek to be accepting and welcoming places. It is considered to be rude or even "unchristian" to be confrontational about another's behavior.

2) Congregations are volunteer organizations. As such, they have limited authority or means to address inappropriate behavior.

3) Congregations are eager to survive, especially when they are not growing. Therefore, they are fearful of "offending" regular members.

4) Because it is often difficult to find individuals willing to accept leadership positions in congregations, individuals with personality disorders often find an opportunity in congregations to exercise power and influence, which they are unable to do in other areas of their life.

5) Though seminaries do some screening of candidates, including psychological testing, personality disorders don't always show up on the tests that are used.

6) Pastors are seldom trained to identify personality disorders.

7) Because individuals with personality disorders are often able to function quite normally with everyday tasks and do not exhibit the kinds of symptoms that are usually diagnosed as mental health problems, it is often mistakenly assumed that they will respond appropriately to rational or biblical suggestions and admonitions.

We will take a closer looks at personality disorders, how to recognize them, and the best ways to manage them in congregational settings. But we need to answer another question before we get there. Some may already be thinking, "My congregation is neither a clinic nor a treatment center. My job is not to practice psychology, and even if I were to try, I wouldn't be very good at it. My task is proclaiming God's Word. What does any of this have to do with theology?" The next chapter is an attempt to explain why the ability to work with different kinds of personalities is theologically important and how it relates to the purpose of the church.

5 A THEOLOGY OF RELATIONSHIPS

Working with individuals with personal disorders in a congregational setting requires a theology of relationships.

I have in recent times, whenever the opportunity presented itself, conducted an informal survey, asking, "When in your life have you felt closest to God?" As one might expect, people describe a variety of experiences. Some talk about the time when they went through a difficult illness and felt sustained by the presence of Christ. Others felt God's presence most intently at the death and funeral of a loved one. Still others describe an intimate encounter with God while they were on a spiritual retreat or while they contemplated the beauty of the world around them.

These experiences are readily understandable, and most of us can identify with them, as we have had similar experiences. If I had asked the question of myself, my first response would have been, "The time of the birth of my first child." That experience was so miraculous, so awe-inspiring, that there has been none other in my lifetime that has even come close to comparing with it.

Still, what I find surprising is that as often as I have asked that question, I have yet to have someone describe to me an experience of forgiving or being forgiven. I find that curious. After all, isn't that at the heart and core of the Christian religion? Isn't forgiveness one of the most distinctive features of Christianity—a belief and practice different from most other world religions? Isn't the cross the ultimate symbol of our faith? I'm not sure I can ever hope to fully comprehend the meaning of the crucifixion of Jesus, but this much is clear, it has something to do with relationships. It has to do with my relationship with God, and quite possibly also my relationship with others, and both of these relationships have something to do with forgiveness. Why is it then, that typically when we try to think of times when we feel "closest to God," solitary experiences are what come easily to mind, while relational experiences, especially the experience of forgiving and being forgiving, seldom do?

Faith

Religion provides a believer with a particular world view, a philosophy, a way of life. It supplies a framework for understanding oneself, one's purpose in life, the nature of God, and the ultimate destiny of history. As such, it has a certain content that can be taught and transmitted. Thus, *faith* can be used as a noun: "This is my faith" or "Faith of our Fathers." It can be the answer to "what," as in, "Tell me *what* you believe." Much of congregational life, including the sermons on Sundays, Bible studies, and Sunday School classes, centers around this task of teaching content. Unfortunately, the impression is sometimes given that the process of mastering a certain body of information and giving one's assent to it is the essence of religion. That perhaps is one of the reasons for a large drop-off in attendance after children reach adulthood. Once you have learned the content, what other reason is there to continue to go to church? But to assume that belief is a matter of becoming informed, as one might learn the traditions, history, and statistics of a sport team, is to completely misunderstand faith. Belief and knowledge are not the same.

By far the most frequent use of *faith* in the New Testament is as a verb. As a verb, faith is not a thing so much as it is an action. And, as a verb, it means not merely giving assent to something—as in believing *that* something is true—as believing *in* something, making a commitment to it. It implies an act of trust, a letting go of individual certainty and relying upon something that can't be proven. It is like Indiana Jones in *The Last Crusade,* who, only after stepping off the cliff at the edge of the abyss, discovers that his foot lands on something solid.

Thus far, most religious teachers, I believe, would be fully on board with me. However, I would argue this still is an incomplete description of faith and misses a vital ingredient. What the New Testament teaches is not simply "belief in" but "belief into."

There is a peculiarity in the Greek language that brings this out. Throughout the New Testament, the verb for "believe" is followed by the preposition εις, which means "into." Because it sounds clumsy in English to say "he believed into Christ," it is regularly translated as if the preposition were εν, "in"—"he believed in Christ," and the difference is dismissed as an idiosyncrasy of language. But the original language conveys a concept that should not be overlooked. Believing, in the New Testament, is characterized not by trust in a set of principles but by trust in a person. In other words, it involves entering *into* a relationship. Thus, "believing into" is not that dissimilar from falling in love. It involves "letting go." It feels often like surrender. When one believes, one enters *into* a relationship with that person, and the relationship itself becomes more important than the content. This often is experienced as passing through a doorway, beginning a new chapter, entering into a new experience, or finding oneself in a new world.

When faith is viewed solely as a noun, the temptation exists to measure it solely by its content. Is it correct? Is it a truthful restatement? When faith is a noun, one can make attempts to capture and contain it accurately. Believers are those who acknowledge the truthfulness of the content of faith and derive a sense of certitude from having done so. That certitude can lead easily to a compulsion, possibly even a fanaticism, to defend the truth and to make judgments about those whose faith content appears lacking.

When faith becomes a verb, it still has content, but there is a reordering of priorities. The truthfulness of the content has become secondary to another truth—the dynamics of the relationship.

Congregations as Relational Communities of Faith

In common usage, the attribution "Christian" has become the normative way of describing one who believes in Christ. Whether that is expressed as "being born again," "having saving faith," "turning one's life over to Christ," or "believing in Jesus as your personal Savior," the purpose of the church is frequently seen as ancillary to the primary goal of making Christians, whether that purpose if fulfilled through the teaching of the training evangelists, by serving as an incubator for new Christians, or by being a storage place for mature Christians where they can be shelved until their time comes to enter the kingdom of heaven. One would assume there is substantial biblical support for that viewpoint. In actuality, however, once one begins to look, it is hard to miss the fact that "church" in the New Testament is not an accidental and possibly optional byproduct of religious experience but rather is central to Christianity.

This is unfortunate, as the term "to be a Christian" is rarely used in the New Testament. When it does occur, it is used by non-Christians. Luke observes that it was in Antioch that followers of the way were first described as "Christians." Thus, it was not a self-attribution but an attribution applied to them by their fellow citizens in Antioch, probably because mostly what they knew about them was that they tended to talk a lot about Christ. Similarly, Herod Agrippa, who out of curiosity wanted to hear what the prisoner Paul had to say about this new religion he had heard something about, concludes somewhat dismissively by saying, "You almost persuade me in becoming a Christian." However, when believers in the New Testament describe themselves, they are far more apt to use words like "saints," "followers of the way," or "disciples." Even more frequently, followers of Jesus are simply described as "in Christ": "If anyone is in Christ, he is a new creation" (II Cor. 5:17).

By their preferred use of the attribution "in Christ," the New Testament writers were emphasizing that believing meant entering into relationships—both with Christ and with fellow believers. Both relationships involve a letting go, a cognitive humility, a willingness to recognize that one's own way of making sense out of the world is incomplete. Entering into a relationship with God means leaving behind the certainty that can be completely captured or contained in factual statements. It is a dynamic world of relationship filled with both disappointment and delight, with mystery and experience, with wonderment and hope. The same is true of the relationships that develop among the diversity of people called together by Christ. Both relationships—the one with God and the one with fellow believers—involve an element of trust, a willingness to become vulnerable. And both result in experiencing oneself in a new way. Thus, belief in the New Testament sense is far from the concept of accepting a set of principles that are to be studied and followed as well as from the idea that spirituality is a solitary pursuit best experienced on one's own. The clear implication is that one cannot have a relationship with Jesus Christ without also having a relationship with other believers.

The Body of Christ

The New Testament writers employ a number of vivid images in an attempt to describe their understanding of "church." Among others, church is depicted as the bride of Christ, as a building of living stones, and as a royal priesthood. But perhaps the most vivid and dynamic is that the church is the body of Christ.

Paul elaborates this analogy extensively in I Corinthians 12. Several points become clear from his amplification:

The body is made of up many diverse elements. "Are all an ear?" Paul asks rhetorically. One cannot create a body without diversity. When, therefore, advocates argue that congregations ought to develop a mission plan that focuses upon people like themselves, since that is the way they are most likely to be successful, one must ask: Successful at what? When it comes to replication, cancerous tissue is also successful, capable of growing far more rapidly than noncancerous, differentiated, tissue. There is much to be feared in creating communities of like-appearing and like-minded believers, as these can often become the breeding grounds for narrow-mindedness and bigotry.

Congregations have, in many cases, fallen far short of achieving the kind of diversity that the Scriptures uplift. Still, to be fair, it is worth noting that for all their shortcomings, churches are still one of the few places in society where both young and old, rich and poor, educated and uneducated frequently gather. As a parish pastor, I often marveled that in the same day I could make a pastoral call at a home in the country club area of town, be greeted at the door by a maid, and be ushered into a room filled with expensive furnishings, where, with the assistance of home health care, I could converse with a genteel octogenarian recovering from surgery, while a few hours earlier, I had been sitting on the front steps of the church, entering into a conversation with a homeless person who had offered me a drink from his bottle in a paper sack.

And neither I nor they felt out of place in these encounters.

In addition, *the body analogy emphasizes entering into significant partnerships with fellow believers.* In describing how the parts fit together, Paul writes how "God has combined the members of the body" (I Cor. 12:24). These are not people who have no more contact with one another beyond the happenstance of occasionally occupying the same place at the same time. These are people whose talents and differences have drawn them together. Their differences are essential. They are drawn together not by similarities but by diversity. They confront one another. They complement each other. Together they, in some way, become complete. As a whole, they become more than just the sum of their parts.

There is also the acknowledgment that *at various times, some are worthy of more honor than others.* Group goals, the goals of the kingdom, are more important than individual goals, and those who have done the most to extend the kingdom's goals are recognized. Yet, at the same time, the value and worth of each and every member is upheld, with the "least in the kingdom of heaven" also honored as the "greatest."

No part of the body has a separate existence apart from its role in the body. One of the most sickening images of warfare is the sight of disconnected body parts. A human organ that has such grace and beauty when part of the body is gruesome when found separated from it. Not only does this analogy indicate the lifelessness and tragedy of a separate existence, it also highlights the loss that the body feels when missing a vital part. To be a part of the body is to frequently experience grief over the barriers and separation that arise between people.

And ultimately, *the body is united under the head of Jesus.* There is a commonality of purpose that brings all the parts together. This unity of purpose bridges all other differences. Strikingly, when Paul employs this body image, he doesn't write of the need of the different parts to love each other or even to like each other, but rather, because God has "combined the members of the body," to "honor" those "we think as less honorable" and to "have equal concern for each other" (vv.23-24). A certain respect grows out of being joined with others in a common purpose. One sees it often in reunions that are held for veterans as well as for graduating classes. At the time they were joined together in pursuing a common goal, differences of personality may have created petty irritations and annoyances, but from the perspective of time, their shared experiences become treasured memories. Differences became less sources of conflict and more often an opportunity to show honor and respect. Likewise, those brought together in congregations find a unity in their purpose. Merely the process of being together, rubbing shoulders with one another, and sometimes irritating one another, leads to a depth of relationships and of religious experience that cannot be replicated by individual spirituality.

Given the fullness with which Paul elaborates the analogy of the body of Christ and what it means to be "in Christ," it appears to be a keystone for him in the manner in which he addresses various aspects of church life. In writing to the church in Corinth, expulsion from the body becomes the form of discipline that he urges the Corinthians to exercise when it comes to dealing with an individual living with his father's wife (I Cor. 5:1-13). It also becomes the theological underpinning of the celebration of the Lord's Supper. After upbraiding the Corinthians for their selfish and chaotic manner of celebrating the meal, he reminds them of Christ's institution of this practice, encourages self-examination before participation, and says that "anyone who eats of the bread and drinks without recognizing the body of the Lord eats and drinks judgment on himself" (I Cor. 11:29). Some theologians have interpreted this to refer to the real presence of Christ in the sacrament. In the context, however, with Paul's detailed elaboration of the concept of the body of Christ in the following chapter and the specific mention of "the body of the Lord" without a corresponding mention of "the blood of the Lord" (despite the inclusion of "drinks" with "eats"), this appears to uplift the importance of recognizing and affirming the relationships that exist "in Christ" as part of the significance and meaning of this meal.

In many congregations, the celebration of Communion also becomes an opportune time to reflect on the relationships with all those who have gone before. In Hebrews 12:1, a "great cloud of witnesses" is depicted, cheering on those who are still running the race. The celebration of the banquet of the Lord, which is a foretaste of the things to come, becomes also an occasion to look back in remembrance of those who have completed the race. Understanding how faith brings us into community extends relationships far beyond today into the remembered past and to the hopeful future.

Overcoming Obstacles

Thus far, the image of a congregation is alluring. Many are drawn to congregations as a place where they hope to experience acceptance, support, encouragement, and friendship. Unfortunately, it is often the failure to experience any of those that has led to many to jettison any connection with congregations.

Neither a relationship with God or with others is a simple matter. They may begin simply enough, but both are likely to encounter extreme obstacles that must be overcome if they are to grow and become mature.

A great deal of Scripture is focused upon the difficulty of God's task of reestablishing a relationship with his fallen creation. The relationship doesn't exist because we have so much in common. On the contrary: the lack of any common ground makes this the most mystifying relationship of all. There seems to be no reason that God should be interested in us. It is not love at first sight. As much as we might like to take some credit, based upon the hope and desire that God might pay some attention to us, it is clear that anything we have contributed to the relationship, other than response to his gracious gift, is at best only a hindrance. Passages like Philippians 2 and Hebrews 2 expound on the sacrifice and humility required of God in order to reconcile the world unto himself.

This is a relationship so difficult that it can be entered into only by faith, which ultimately requires of us the most difficult task of all: letting go.

The task of loving others follows in the path of forgiveness and reconciliation that he paved for us. This does nothing to earn favor in God's sight. However, it does have something to do with making Christ present in this world. "Whatever you did for one of the least of these brothers of mine, you did for me" (Mt. 25:40).

An emphasis upon the church as the place where significant relationships come into being is found throughout the parables and teachings of Jesus. When Jesus sought out the two fishermen, Simon and Andrew, to become disciples, he invited them: "Come, follow me, and I will make you fishers of men" (Mk 1:17). Countless sermons and evangelism campaigns have been based on this passage, most connecting the call to become a disciple with the expectation that one must also be a witness. Believers have been taught how to "go fishing," equipping them with testimonies and methods for proclaiming the Gospel in their individual relationships with people. The image was that of fishing as we know it—with a pole, a line, and a bobber—and often enough, it seemed like the bait was something deceptive, something that would lure people close enough to set the hook.

But the kind of fishing that the disciples did was not with a pole and a line. They were fishing with nets, and at the time Jesus spoke with them, they were in the process of mending their nets. One who fishes with nets doesn't catch fish one by one. A net is cast over a wide arc and brings all within that arc closer together.

This becomes explicitly clear in the parable of the dragnet (Mt. 13:47-50). The net brings together good fish and bad. The express point of the parable is that it isn't up to the fishermen to decide who belongs and who doesn't. The task of the fisherman is simply to cast the net and draw it in. The ultimate community of God may come into being only in the future, but it is already being brought into being in the present and will continue to grow.

A similar theme is found in many other of the parables about the kingdom. In the parable of the mustard seed, the tiny seed not only grows exponentially into a large tree, but in doing so, it becomes a place where all the birds of the air come together (Mt. 13:31-32).

When Jesus promises, "Where two or three come together in my name, there am I with them" (Mt 18:20), one could almost conclude that a solitary religious experience would be devoid of the presence of Christ. Whether or not such a conclusion is justified, what is clear is that in context, these words are about the issue of forgiveness, and Jesus implies that forgiveness is always two-dimensional. Sin disrupts not only one's relationship with God but also with the community of believers. The act of forgiveness, therefore, must also involve members of the community to which one belongs as well as God.

Reading these passages, one could easily become dismayed, for many congregations today seem to fall far short of the kind of ideal Jesus describes. Yet, we are reminded that from a divine perspective, congregations are always more significant than they outwardly appear. One of the most beautiful depictions of this is found in John's vision at the beginning of Revelation. John describes how he was spoken to by one "like a son of man." This awe-inspiring figure is described as having hair as white as wool, with eyes like a blazing fire and a voice like the sound of rushing waters. But he is observed standing in the midst of seven lampstands. The seven lampstands, it becomes clear, represent each of the seven churches to which John is asked to write. The letters to these churches detail many of their faults: that they have "forsaken their first love," that they tolerate false teaching, that they are neither "hot nor cold." Yet, as John watches, these congregations, represented by flickering candles on lampstands—near but clearly separate from the one "like a son of man" standing in their midst—they morph into something entirely different: bright stars grasped tightly in God's hand (Rev. 1:16). The imagery is striking. Congregations may be imperfect, but they are where Christ is present, and seen from God's perspective, they shine like stars.

Nearly all congregations include individuals with personality disorders. Sometimes these individuals create conflict, cause misunderstandings, bring about hurt feelings, resist care, or pose difficult challenges to relationships, causing the hopeful light that a congregation desires to hold out to the world to be at best a guttering candle. Yet, it is in community that these individuals are best cared for, and in community that these individuals can best offer their unique contributions to others. Grasped in God's hands the light of congregations grow bright. Growth in understanding personality disorders by both pastors and congregations can be a significant asset in practicing a theology of relationships.

6 DIAGNOSING PERSONALITY DISORDERS

The purpose of diagnosis is not labeling but "knowing" (literally, the word means "to know thoroughly"). Recognizing a pattern and knowing that there is a name for it can reduce confusion and the feeling of being overwhelmed that often accompanies the relationship with a personality-disordered individual. The ultimate purpose of this "knowing thoroughly" is care. Diagnosis leads to being able to devise a method of communication and response that can lead to better interactions with the individual and for the health of the congregation as a whole.

Official diagnosis of personality disorders should be left to the mental health professionals who are trained in the diagnostic criteria and whose experience has involved working with many. An informal diagnosis, however, may be useful if one suspects that a congregational member may have a personality disorder.

There are a few general characteristics that may indicate that the person you are observing has a personality disorder.

1.) The patterns you are observing have repeated over a period of time. A personality disorder is *enduring*. It involves not just one instance but many.

2.) The pattern is pervasive. It will occur not just in your relationship with the individual but across a broad range of personal and social situations.

3.) The pattern involves both the way the individual thinks— how he or she perceives, experiences, and interprets the world—and his or her external behavior: the methods the individual employs to achieve his or her intentions.

4.) The pattern differs significantly from the expectation of the individual's "culture"—that is, it is different from the way you would anticipate most people would think or act. Others most likely consider this person's behavior as "uncivil," "offensive," or "odd."

5.) The pattern in these individuals involves two or more areas of function:

–Thinking: their ways of perceiving and viewing themselves and others and events.

–Feeling: their emotional range, its intensity, stability, or appropriateness.

–Relationships: the style and nature of their relationships with others.

–Impulse control: their ability to restrain, delay, filter, or mange impulses.

6.) The pattern leads to significant distress or impairment in:

–Social areas, such as their marriage, friendship, family, and acquaintances.

–Occupational areas, such as their relationships with the bosses, coworkers, employees, customers, and clients.

–Areas of life skills, such as finances, planning, safety, and legalities.

7.) The pattern is not better accounted for by another mental health condition, such as depression, anxiety, or mania.

8.) The pattern is not better accounted for by the effects of drug abuse, steroids, or medication complications. Individuals with personality disorders are known to have a higher incidence of substance abuse issues than the general population, but when these two overlap, the substance abuse issues should be dealt with first.

9.) The pattern is not better accounted for by a medical condition, such as a head trauma, seizures, or dementia.

Another way of looking at this is to be mindful of the three characteristics to a personality disorder. First, they lack an observing ego—the ability to self-reflect; they appear to be unaware that they are in any way contributing to the difficulty of relationships and typically ascribe any problems that are occurring to the actions of others. This contributes to the durability of the pattern. Secondly, they have a limited set of functional defenses and coping skills and therefore are vulnerable, easily hurt, or threatened. Thirdly, they will often utilize a drama pattern instead of a problem-solving pattern when dealing with difficulties.

The Drama Pattern

"Oh, so you're the new pastor? Welcome to our Improv Theater. You won't need a script. You won't need to be skilled at method acting. You don't even need to know in advance what your role is supposed to be. Just react to what goes on around you, and you will soon discover what it is and act accordingly. You will find you can play your part quite naturally."

Most pastors of congregations at some time or another have had the puzzling feeling like they had taken on a role in a play. They had suddenly become a character that was very much unlike themselves. Others saw them as "stubborn," when they saw themselves as overly placating. Or others saw them as lacking empathy, when they saw themselves as deeply caring. Or others saw them as "offensive" when they saw themselves as being likable and outgoing.

Of course, some of the roles a pastor is given are useful, even though they are far removed from reality. It is not uncommon to be placed on a pedestal. After all, the pastor does represent God, and because of that representation, they often can bring God's presence into a hospital room or a funeral mortuary.

But the dramas we are talking about are not simply a matter of projection. They are the dramas created by personality disorders.

Most people, if they encounter a problem, will go through a form of problem solving. If, for example, you are a pastor and people are complaining that you are not spending enough time in the office, you might begin by reflecting upon what that means. Does it mean that they don't know what you do with your time, or that they think you are not working hard enough, or that they would like you to be more available to people? You would then consider possible actions in response. You might abide by their suggestions and keep published office hours. Or you might try to find ways to more effectively communicate your goals and priorities and the portion of time you allot to each. Or you might decide to make known the times you spend in a local coffee shop and invite people to come and join you there. You then select which action you think is the most appropriate—implement it, evaluate it, and make adjustments as needed.

A person with a personality disorder, however, frequently has an impaired process for problem solving. The goal of the process is not producing solutions and adaptations but in defending and validating one's identity. Not having a clear picture of oneself—an "observing ego"—the individual repetitively uses life experiences to affirm a self-image.

Dating back to the 1960s, Stephen Karpman, in his book *Fairy Tales and Script Drama Analysis,* first described the "drama triangle." He argued that the three stereotypical roles often found in fairy tales and melodramas are very similar to the psychological roles that individuals often assume in a problem situation. Basing the roles on characters like Dudley-Do-Right, Little Nell, and Snidely Whiplash, he named them "The Rescuer," "The Victim," and "The Persecutor." The Karpman Drama Triangle, as noted by Dr. Greg Lester, a widely known lecturer about the care and management of personality disorders, fairly accurately described the dramas created by and around individuals with personality disorders.

A *rescuer* is one who sees himself or herself as caring and compassionate. In religious terms, this is the role of "savior" or "martyr." These individuals often believe that their own needs are unimportant and thus subjugate their own needs for those of others. Full of good intentions, they believe that they exist primarily to help others. However, they often fail to see how much they are driven by their own need to gain approval to increase their feelings of self-worth. Thus, a rescuer may often prove to be entirely unhelpful. When rescuers see the other person as helpless and incompetent and in need of a rescuer's skills in order to survive, they feed dependency and a greater sense of helplessness. They are then often surprised when their "sacrificial" care is met with either manipulation or lack of appreciation.

Rescuers have a lot to gain from this role. They are usually viewed as "good people" and receive admiration from family, friends, and community for their selfless giving to others. But it comes at the cost of their own feelings, thoughts, and actions. They consistently suppress their own needs for those of others and seem unable to stand up for and ask directly for what they need. Thus, they are often overworked and tired and prime candidates for burnout.

Victims believe that they are unable to care for themselves. In religious terms, this is the role of a sinner—at least in the sense of someone who feels hopeless, helpless, and ashamed. They, however, tend to deny responsibility for themselves and feel incapable of even trying to avoid failure.

The primary sense here is vulnerability. Sometimes their sense of helplessness is a result of misfortune or something that has been done to them. Sometimes it is the feeling of inadequacy or having failed to measured up to the standards of others. Everyone needs support at some time in their life. For victims, it is their way of life. They use their dependence to connect to others and keep them tied to them. They are adept at offering the gratitude and appreciation that rescuers crave, but they are also adept at utilizing persecutors, entering and reentering abusive relationships in order to justify and demonstrate their dependency needs.

Depression is often the price that a victim pays for the continual helplessness and hopelessness that must be perpetuated in order to maintain the role.

Persecutors see themselves as acting to make the world right. In religious terms, this is the role of the judge. They believe they know the truth and feel an obligation to use the power of truth to set others straight. They justify their actions as, "I'm correcting." They see those who do not go along with their corrections as victims— people who feel sorry for themselves instead of accepting the solution that was offered.

Though it may not always at first be evident, the role of a persecutor originates in shame. Fearing their own inadequacies, these individuals build themselves up by tearing others down. They compensate for their own flaws by focusing on those of others. They have a strong sense of what is "moral," "just," "fair," and "right" (as it applies to others) and punish those who they perceive are in violation of these values.

The benefit for persecutors is being able to deny their own inadequacies by focusing on everyone else's. The price they pay is to go through life agitated and angry most of the time. Unable to acknowledge their softer, more vulnerable side, they are incomplete persons. All of their energy is dedicated to being outraged, which keeps others at a distance.

The Karpman Drama Triangle describes a relationship matrix in which interactions feed off of the feelings and needs of another to fuel a self-identity. Victims validate their sense of vulnerability by getting pity from rescuers and blame from the persecutors. The rescuers validate their image as self-sacrificing martyrs by getting criticism from the persecutors and appreciation from the victims. The persecutors validate their image as the righteous ones by blaming victims for not being willing to help themselves and by blaming the rescuers for their naiveté and lack of ability to stand up for themselves. These are relationships that are caught up in a continual push-and-pull power struggle: a game that seeks to manipulate others into a desired opposing role. Guilt, manipulation, enabling, resentment, blaming, and shaming are the rules of this game. No one gets better.

However, the roles in the Drama Triangle aren't necessarily fixed. Individuals can sometimes occupy more than one role at the same time and frequently switch roles, compelling others around them to do so likewise. Thus, the Drama Triangle frequently becomes a dance with dizzying twists and sudden turns.

Let's take the example of a Pastor Merciful, who comes to the rescue of Mr. Hopeless, a homeless man who originally stopped by the church asking for a handout. There is a compliant and appreciative attitude about Mr. Hopeless, unlike some of the demanding vagrants who sometimes came to the church door, and after several visits, Pastor Merciful gets involved, wanting to do more for Mr. Hopeless than simply provide a temporary handout, which did nothing to address his homeless status. So, Pastor Merciful begins to spend time with Mr. Hopeless, getting to know a little of his background and making telephone calls to identify resources that might be of benefit to him. Meanwhile, Mr. Righteous, a member of the church board, begins to complain about the amount of time Pastor Merciful is wasting on people like Mr. Hopeless, while members of Pastor Merciful's congregation are not receiving the attention they deserve. Thus, Pastor Merciful, who was initially a rescuer for Mr. Hopeless has now also become a victim to Mr. Righteous, the persecutor.

Now let's suppose that in an effort to give Mr. Hopeless the chance to earn some money rather than receive handouts, Pastor Merciful assigns Mr. Hopeless some part-time tasks around the church, for which he is paid. One day, he is asked to pick up some needed items from the local hardware store. Since Mr. Hopeless doesn't have a car, Pastor Merciful lends him the keys to her car. Mr. Hopeless does not return. Having had enough of this game of people trying to fix his problems with nickels and dimes when he knows it calls for more than any can afford, Mr. Hopeless takes the pastor's car to another state. Having begun as a victim, Mr. Hopeless has now become a persecutor, transforming Pastor Merciful, the rescuer, into the role of victim. Meanwhile, Mr. Righteous, hearing what has happened, steps into assist in locating the missing car and returning it to its owner. Having begun as a persecutor, he now enters the role of rescuer to come to the aid of his victimized pastor, Pastor Merciful.

Most people at one time or another have found themselves playing one or more of these roles in a relational matrix. But for individuals with personality disorders, these roles are not simply occasional experiences but a way of life. Lacking flexibility, they are often locked into these roles. It is as if they were objects made of hard plastic and, when pressed into a confined space with others who are more flexible, like objects made of foam, shape them into roles and patterns that fit them. The basic shape of a personality disorder creates a distinct and recognizable pattern, and, as we shall see, the type of personality disorder you encounter can often be determined by what role the individual is playing when he or she first creates the drama and the subsequent role to which he or she may have switched. The switch and the consequent drama roles assigned to others serve to affirm the basic view of life this person holds about himself or herself and others. But it does nothing to resolve a problem.

In the example above about a pastor being asked to increase office hours, a pastor with a personality disorder, instead of attempting to find a solution to the concern that was expressed, will take the request for more office hours personally and consider it an attack. That pastor will see himself or herself as a rescuer but will now enter the role of victim. His or her reactions and behaviors are justified and rationalized, while the original problem remains unaddressed and possibly amplified. Additional problems are created.

When personality disorders occur in congregations, the stage is set not just for an interaction between two people—but between many. Thus, even if you manage to recognize the drama roles being assigned and manage to extract yourself, it does not mean that others will not be caught up in it. Dramas are powerful interactions and have a way of producing endless sequels: *Superman* most recently reappeared as *Superman V*. Still, it is much more enjoyable to watch the show from the audience than from the stage.

The Ten Personality Disorders

The *DSM-5* describes ten different personality disorders. Some of the names, like "dependent" and "avoidant" quite aptly and accurately describe the pattern of traits that make up a certain type of personality. Other names, however, like "schizotypal" and "borderline" are mystifying and archaic, imported from the archives of the early years of psychiatry. They need explanation and amplification to be understood. Still others, like "obsessive-compulsive" and "paranoid" are misleading, because they can be confused with similar sounding-mental health issues or have changed in meaning over time.

The *DSM-5* groups the ten disorders into three clusters, according to certain similarities.

Cluster A personalities include paranoid, schizoid, and

schizotypal. In general, these describe individuals with odd or eccentric behavior. In a congregational setting, these are personality types that provide challenges for assimilation. Paranoid personality disorder is distinguished from "paranoia," which often includes delusions and hallucinations, and describes a more general attitude of distrust and suspiciousness. "Schizoid" derives from a Greek word meaning "to split." Is was used originally to describe someone whose exaggerated tendency to direct attention to one's inner life led to being "split" off from one's external world. "Schizotypal" is a word originally coined to describe an individual whose eccentric behavior and modes of thinking at times somewhat resemble someone with schizophrenia—but who is not schizophrenic. As we shall see, these are individuals in a congregational setting that provide "challenges for inclusiveness."

Cluster B personalities include antisocial, borderline, histrionic, and narcissistic. In general, these are individuals who create chaos and drama in their interpersonal relationships. In a congregational context, these are personality types that often create conflict and turmoil. "Antisocial" describes individuals who typically don't abide by social norms. "Borderline" was a word originally coined to describe individuals who "walked the line" between exhibiting psychotic symptoms such as hearing voices, and neurotic symptoms such as anxiety and depression. They are now seen primarily as individuals with attachment issues. "Histrionic" describes individuals who often utilize exaggerated actions and emotions, much like an actor on a stage. "Narcissistic" derives from the Greek myth of the same name and describes a person overly concerned about "image." These are individuals who, in a congregational setting, provide "challenges for management."

Cluster C personalities include avoidant, dependent, and obsessive-compulsive. In general, these are individuals characterized by anxiousness in their relationships with others. In a congregational setting, these are personality types that often appear on the surface to be good members but whose real needs are often not identified. "Avoidant" and "dependent" are personality types whose name aptly describe their characteristics. Obsessive-compulsive personality disorder (OCPD) should be distinguished from obsessive-compulsive disorder (OCD). The latter is more typically characterized by repetitive hand washing or excessive checking of locks. OCPD describes a more pervasive pattern of preoccupation with perfectionism and control. In a congregational setting, these are individuals who provide "challenges to meaningful care."

The following chapters will detail each of these ten personality disorders in greater detail: first, by providing several "snapshots" of the personality disorder and style as it has occurred in a congregational life, followed by a general description of both the disorder and the style, and finally, with a description of the drama pattern typically employed by that disorder.

The snapshots are based upon real incidents, though names and places have been changed, some details altered or omitted, and, in some cases, several examples conflated into one story. *In most of these snapshots, not enough information is provided to determine whether there is sufficient severity, durability, and pervasiveness to warrant a diagnosis of a personality disorder as opposed to a personality style, but the traits described illustrate characteristic features of this personality.*

In addition to drawing from the official diagnostic criteria of the *DSM-5*, the general descriptions utilize information provided in *A Handbook of Diagnosis and Treatment of DSM-IV-TR Personality Disorders (Second Edition)* by Len Sperry and in *Power with People: How to Handle Just about Anyone to Accomplish Just About Anything* by Gregory Lester. Both are highly recommended for anyone desiring to deepen their knowledge of personality disorders.

The drama patterns, as you will see, are important for understanding the techniques for management and care for personality disorders described in chapter seventeen.

7 PARANOID PERSONALITY
(CLUSTER A—ODD PARISHIONERS, CHALLENGES TO ASSIMILATION)

Snapshots

The congregation had entered into a building project, a remodeling of the educational wing originally built in the 1950s. The remodel involved an almost complete gutting of the interior of the building to enable rewiring and plumbing and a restructuring of the rooms.

The project was running behind schedule. With the pastor's permission, the contractor was given the okay to continue work on Sundays.

Parishioners, though, had difficulty finding places to park as construction vehicles occupied portions of the parking lot. Hallways were tracked with sheetrock-dust footprints. The sanctuary was entered by pushing through plastic sheeting hung to keep out the dust from that part of the building. Every now and then, the singing of hymns and the message of the sermon were punctuated with a loud and startling crash echoing from the adjacent wing. People complained.

Louise thought that she had a good idea. On Monday morning, she called the pastor and suggested that maybe the workers might be invited to join them for worship, taking just an hour off from their labors. She was quite proud of this proposed solution, which she believed would be a win-win for everyone involved. The pastor was wary. Even though he was appreciative of her attempt to find a workable solution to their problem and told her so, on two previous occasions Louise had resigned from committees on which she had served when her ideas had not been accepted. It seemed that once she had arrived at a potential solution to a problem or a subject under discussion, there were no other possible alternatives. She became rigid and demanding, and if unable to prevail, she would simply walk out. He knew that despite her optimism in this case, her idea most likely wouldn't work. He tried to explain the reasons the contractor probably wouldn't agree to it: he wouldn't want it to be seen as forcing religion on his workers; in many cases, the workers couldn't just stop in the middle of something just because it was time for church; and either he would have to pay them for just sitting around idly for an hour, or his workers would have to extend their day by an hour without overtime pay, which wouldn't please them.

Louise was incensed, particularly since her pastor wasn't even willing to broach the subject with the contractor. She fumed about it for the next several days to anyone who would listen, and within two weeks, she had transferred her membership to another congregation.

***

First Presbyterian Church is an urban congregation in a large metropolitan area. At one time the area was inhabited by wealthy immigrants who built large Queen Anne, Colonial, and Victorian-style homes. Many of these were now crumbling and in a state of disrepair, but the area had been declared a historic district to encourage restoration and to maintain the unique nature of the neighborhood. One of the homes in need of repair was owned by the congregation and had once served as a parsonage. When pastors began living in their own homes, the building, for a time, was used for educational space before eventually being divided into apartment space and rented.

The building, however, needed continual maintenance. The congregation couldn't afford to pay for a regular caretaker, and volunteers were not always available or willing to respond to the needs when they arose. Once, after a heavy rain, one of the renters complained about water pouring out from one of the light fixtures. It was evident that the building was unsafe and could no longer be rented until repairs were done—repairs that included both a new slate roof (a requirement of the historic district) and a complete rewiring of the electrical system.

The congregation, needing to do repairs of its own historic church building, could not afford the necessary work. The only option seemed to be to sell the building—not an attractive option not only because of the loss of a historic part of the church but also because of the loss of needed parking space (some of the space used for church parking was on the lot belonging to this house).

The pastor was thus overwhelmed with joy when one day she received a letter from a philanthropic institution indicating interest in the building. Its leaders believed that by restoring the building, they could help stabilize the neighborhood and encourage additional investment. They offered to do the needed work at no cost to the congregation. The building would continue to be owned by the congregation, and they could continue to utilize the parking spaces. The only thing they asked in return was the opportunity to use the building for their own office space rent free for a period of twenty years.

It was like a gift from heaven. She indicated that the congregation was definitely interested and asked that the necessary documents be drawn up.

On the day of the signing, the president of the congregation, Wilber Renshaw, went with her to meet the officials of the philanthropic organization. He was a man who had grown up in the congregation, had never married, and lived in a small house nearby with his mother, where he had lived all of his life. He had put on an ill-fitting suit for the occasion.

Five members of the philanthropic organization met them when they arrived. Several of them were well-known community leaders. The pastor and Wilber were greeted with warm smiles, which were reciprocated by the pastor, who began to thank them for their generous offer. Wilber, however, hung back.

When it came time to sign, Wilber abruptly said that he didn't sign anything that he hadn't read. They politely mentioned that they had previously sent a draft.

"You're not asking me to sign a draft," Wilber said. "You're asking me to sign this document."

Wilber sat at the table and began to read. Conversation slowly died and came to a halt. The smiles disappeared.

"So what would a building like this normally rent for?" he asked.

One of the philanthropic members offered a figure.

"No way," said Wilber. "I live in this neighborhood. You'd have to pay a lot more than that."

He asked about insurance. He asked about taxes. They pointed him to the places in the document where those items were dealt with. Wilber wasn't satisfied. In the end, he refused to sign. "We need to think this over some more. We need to have a lawyer look it over."

The philanthropic group said okay, but that they needed to have an answer within a month, because, if this wasn't acceptable, they needed to make other plans.

"I don't respond well to pressure," Wilber said. "You're confirming my suspicion that you're trying to pull something over on us."

On the ride back to the church, Wilber went into a long rant about the deceptive practices of high-priced lawyers in their thousand-dollar suits, always trying to pull one over on the little guy. The pastor was at a loss for what to say.

***

The call came late on a Sunday afternoon from a woman who usually sat in one of the back pews of the church and would often leave at the end of the service without greeting anyone. She wore a permanent frown on her face that kept most people at a distance. The pastor knew who she was but didn't know much about her. She seemed like a person who wasn't interested in getting involved, so he pretty much left her to herself.

"When did you start putting 666 on your banners?" she asked that Sunday in the call to the parsonage.

The pastor was taken aback. "What banner? What do you mean?"

"You know exactly what I'm talking about. The 666 on the baptismal banner." A group of ladies made individual banners inscribed with the child's name and the words "Child of God" for each baptism that occurred in church. The banner was hung behind the baptismal font on the day of the baptism, and the family took it home to hang in the child's room after the baptism.

"I still don't know what you mean. There is no 666 on the banner."

"There most certainly was," the caller insisted. The pastor realized that he hadn't actually looked at the banner that morning, but he found it unfathomable that someone, especially the devoted ladies who made those banners, would try to sneak the symbol of the antichrist into church.

The pastor realized that this was an argument that was going nowhere. He finally told her, "If there was, that would certainly have been most inappropriate. I'll check into it."

He still was at a loss to explain the woman's accusation. Was she mentally ill? Had she been hallucinating?

The next day at the office, he called the family of the child who had been baptized and asked if he could have one of the pictures that had been taken of the family group after the baptism, some of which also showed the baptismal banner. When the photo arrived, it was as he thought: it was the typical banner that had been made for all of the baptisms. But then he noted at the bottom of the banner the baptismal symbol that had always been used: three water drops, symbolizing the Trinity. And from a distance, if one really were suspicious and distrustful, it was possible, he supposed, to believe that each of those drops were in the shape of the number six.

***

Randy Wilson was in charge of the audio system at church. He had never been appointed to that position nor had volunteers been sought. He more or less appropriated it as his area of expertise (though in fact he worked as a salesmen in the men's apparel division at a local department store). When the new audio system was installed, he constantly haggled the workmen, insisting that their placement of speakers was all wrong. They were called back three different times to make adjustments. Still, people complained that the system wasn't working right, that there were dead spots where they could hardly hear at all. Randy insisted they didn't know what they were talking about and that they were just a bunch of complainers.

Around this time, there was a tragic death in the congregation—a young father who left behind a widow, a thirteen-year-old son and a nine-year-old daughter. The pastor was particularly concerned about the thirteen-year-old, as even before his father's death, he had been getting into difficulty at school. He didn't seem to have any friends and was often teased. He was a nerdy young man, and his primary interest seemed to be electronics. He delighted in taking things apart to see how they worked.

The pastor thought it might be a good idea for this young man to assist with the sound system at church. It would be a way to give him a sense of belonging as well as a sense of pride. He thought that this would also be a good thing for Randy, as he could take delight in sharing his knowledge with a youngster. He might even become sort of a father figure for him—a relationship that the pastor felt might work both ways, as Randy had no children of his own.

This, however, was a bad idea. Randy was offended at the idea that some "young punk" would mess with his equipment. He immediately bought a cover for all of the equipment so that it could be locked and made inaccessible to anyone else.

It was clear that a mentoring relationship wouldn't work. Still, the pastor thought it a good idea for the young man to be involved. When she talked to him about the possibility, he was very excited and assured her that he knew how it worked. The pastor sought the church council's approval to allow him to run the sound system one Sunday a month.

The first Sunday the young man ran the sound system, everything seemed to work fine. No one seemed to have any difficulty hearing. On the following Sunday, however, when Randy was again running the system, the sound was barely audible. The pastor had to nearly shout in order to be heard. Randy said that it was because the young man had done something to the equipment, and it was no longer working properly. He smugly told anyone who would listen, "I told you this would happen." The pastor, however, suspected that Randy had deliberately kept the volume low as an act of spite.

***

At his invitation, the call committee met in the home of Brett McCann. "We have just the right space for such a meeting," he had said in offering it. Some on the committee wondered what made it "the right space" or why they couldn't just meet at the church, but accepted the invitation anyway. The committee eventually selected Pastor Brian as their next pastor; he would succeed a long-term and much-loved pastor who had finally retired after serving the congregation for fifteen years.

Brett and his wife, Sarah, were the first people to meet Pastor Brian on his arrival and extended a warm and enthusiastic welcome. Brett also presented him with a brick inscribed with his name. Pastor Brian, having heard the adage, "Beware the person who seems too eager to meet the new pastor," wondered how long it would be before this person would also be tossing bricks.

At first, however, things seemed to go well, and Brett, who served on the church council along with his wife, Sarah, who served as the congregational treasurer, was supportive of his ministry. The first sign of trouble came when it came time for annual elections, and Pastor Brian suggested that it was not a good idea for two people from the same household to hold office. Brett chose then not to run again for office while his wife continued as the congregational treasurer (while some said it was still Brett who did all of the accounting). Pastor Brian immediately noted the change in their relationship, as Brett more often than not started to avoid him and from time to time began making critical comments. As Pastor Brian began to learn more of the stories of the congregation, he also began to hear more about Brett's tendencies towards vindictiveness. He often took offense when none was intended and could carry on a grudge for many years.

Brett seemed to become particularly upset at unexpected changes. Though a strong backer of the congregation's Contemporary Service, one Sunday when a modern version of the Lord's Prayer was used instead of the traditional version, he walked out of the service.

Likewise, he seemed far more adept at pointing out ways that new projects would fail than in thinking of possible positive outcomes. When the congregation considered opening a noon time café as a way both to fulfil a local need as well as provide on-the-job training for habitually unemployed individuals in their community, Brett wrote an angry letter to the entire congregation, predicting that the project would fold within a year and complaining that Pastor Brett always seemed more concerned about the "ne'er-do-wells" in their midst than the members of his own congregation.

When Pastor Brian ended his ministry at this congregation, an executive meeting of the church council was convened to conduct an exit interview, Brett walked in uninvited. Not sure what else to do, the congregational president invited his input. He immediately launched into his litany of complaints. Only when one of the newest council members, overcome with her own emotions, interrupted and changed the subject did the meeting get back on course.

General Description

Paranoid Personality Disorder

An individual with paranoid personality disorder exhibits a pervasive pattern of suspiciousness and mistrust of other people. Like a pessimist who always sees the dark side of every picture ("It's a really nice today, isn't it?" "Yeah, but tomorrow it is going to rain again."), an individual with paranoid personality disorder will suspect there may be an ulterior or malevolent motive behind even the most friendly offer. This person views the world as basically a dangerous place and sees himself or herself as mistreated. Others are frequently suspected of having malicious intentions, and therefore these individuals tend to be secretive about their own actions as a protective measure. If someone were to offer an alternative, more positive explanation about the possible motives of another, their suggestions are dismissed out of hand. Once they have arrived at their own conclusion, individuals with a paranoid personality disorder become quite rigid in their beliefs. When they believe they have been wronged, they become vindictive.

These are often thin-skinned individuals who will take nearly everything personally. They view themselves as righteous, and a suggestion about how to do something better will be taken as a personal attack. They often become irritated over even small things. Minor issues become major. The two emotions which they feel with some depth and express with some vehemence are anger and jealousy.

Because it often appears that they are spoiling for a fight and are hypersensitive to both real and imagined slights, others are often wary of them and keep their distance. They have few if any close friends or relationships. Others tend to regard them as cold and argumentative or aloof and humorless.

Their defining issue is a lack of trust. They may cognitively understand biblical passages such as, "Trust in the Lord with all your heart and lean not on your own understanding," but they find that impractical and have abundant reasons to justify why trust in any given situation is not a good idea. In congregations, they frequently become involved, but it is often difficult to find a role for them where their negativity does not create tension.

Paranoid Personality Style

Individuals with paranoid personality style tend to be good listeners, keenly attuned to subtleties of tone or demeanor that may indicate that there are different levels of meaning to what is being said. They are careful in their dealings with others and in confronting new situations and may tend to first see all of the implicit negatives that may arise, but they have learned how to also look for potential positives as well. They are sensitive to criticism but have learned how to assert themselves without becoming overly reactive. They value loyalty and work hard to earn it and retain it.

***

Drama Pattern with Paranoid Personality Disorder

Victim switching to persecutor, switching back to victim, and repeating the cycle.

Individuals with paranoid personality disorder typically begin a drama as vulnerable victims whom other mean-spirited individuals have targeted as an easy mark. They will then, however, quickly switch to becoming the persecutor and judge of their suspected enemies. Their suspiciousness leads them to attack others and accuse them of malevolent intentions. When others respond to this attack, either by counterattacking or by distancing, they once again become victims: "See! I knew you were out to get me!" But feeling once again vulnerable leads to planning acts of retaliation and revenge—a switch back to the persecutor role.

8 SCHIZOID PERSONALITY
(CLUSTER A—ODD PARISHIONERS, CHALLENGES TO ASSIMILATION)

Snapshots

Marvin was a techno geek. He ran a consulting business related to IT issues. He volunteered his services at no cost whenever the congregation experienced issues with its computers or sound system—a contribution that was greatly appreciated.

Marvin liked to share his technical insights with the pastor—conversations that sometimes went on at some length. Because he was appreciative of the work Marvin did, the pastor listened patiently but frankly, at times, was bored by these conversations. He wasn't sure that Marvin was really making all that much with his consulting business as he appeared to live mostly off of his wife's salary.

When the congregation entered into a building project, Marvin again volunteered, this time to do all of the wiring for lighting, sound, and computer access in the new building. It was hard to pass up what looked like a good deal. Unfortunately, Marvin got himself in over his head. By the time someone else was hired to fix the problems that he had created, it cost the congregation an additional $15,000.

Embarrassed, Marvin left the congregation. Shortly thereafter, his wife divorced him. Several times, late on a Saturday night, the pastor received a telephone call from Marvin, wanting to talk about what had happened. He sounded strikingly unemotional about what had happened, discussing it much in the same tone that he used to talk about wiring diagrams. Only slowly did the pastor realize that the technical conversations in which they had engaged had been for Marvin a form of intimacy, and he was now trying to figure out what he was missing.

***

70

He had been abandoned by his mother and raised by his grandmother. He was frequently exterminating himself, putting himself down in some way. He often retreated into intellectualizations. In Bible class, he loved to debate theoretical subjects like: Is the Bible inerrant? Is God loving? Almighty? Omniscient? His questions typically began impersonally: "If one were to think…." "If a person were to say…."

***

"My ideal job," she said, "would be working as a resource librarian in a library where the telephone was broken."

***

Shortly after his graduation from seminary, a great tragedy occurred in the life of Pastor Glenn. He had not yet arrived at his first parish, where he was to assume the duties of an associate pastor, working primarily with the youth ministry. He was driving cross country with his mother and his brother, sleeping in the back seat, when his brother, who was driving, fell asleep. The car went off the road and down an embankment, rolling three times. His mother and his brother were killed. Miraculously, he survived with only minor injuries.

He was advised to take some time before assuming his duties. He decided, however, just one week after the funerals, to go ahead with his installation as associate pastor. The congregation, touched by his tragedy, provided a warm welcome. They provided him with meals. They gave him warm hugs. After a time, however, they began to notice something strange about his response. He thanked them for their kindness and said appropriate words, but there didn't seem to be any depth to it. When asked how he was doing, he would say simply, "Fine." They assumed that he wasn't yet "dealing" with his loss and just needed time.

The senior pastor suggested that doing some counseling might be helpful, and that he would give him some time off if ever he felt that he needed it. He thanked him for the offer but said that at the moment everything was going okay.

Meanwhile, his work didn't seem to be going "okay." Many of the youth of the congregation didn't seem to relate to him. Pastor Glenn was somewhat of an athlete, having played basketball in college, and he enjoyed talking about sports or playing sports with some of the youth. But the youth who were having trouble at school, who were being bullied, who were tempted by drugs, or who weren't getting along with their parents kept their distance. He seemed like an alien in their world. Because he seldom took the time to initiate a conversation with them, some drew the conclusion that he didn't like them.

His sermons were technically and theologically correct. Most of the congregation found them to be mildly boring, though they couldn't always say why. Often they were well researched. However, the examples he offered never seemed true to life. They seemed like imaginary, almost cartoonish characters drawn to illustrate a point, rather than examples from real life from which principles could be drawn.

About six months after his arrival, for the first time he mentioned his own real-life tragedy in a sermon. He used it as an example of the hard times people sometimes go through. Strangely, though, as he told about it, it didn't seem like that much of a hard time.

In the evaluation process after one year, when he was told that some people thought him to be aloof and uncaring, he expressed surprise. He insisted that he cared very deeply about people, and that was one of the main reasons he had gone into ministry.

***

Mary Jane scheduled an appointment for Pastor Richard to meet with her and her husband, Kurt, in the church office. As they sat opposite him, Mary Jane sat on the edge of her seat, gesturing frequently, and often on the verge of tears. Kurt sat rigidly, his face expressionless, at first saying nothing.

Mary Jane began by explaining that her husband has been accused of dealing in child pornography. She didn't know whether or not it was true but thought that Pastor Richard, as their pastor, should know about it, especially since at church, Kurt might be around other children. She explained how police detectives had suddenly shown up at Kurt's office at the university where he taught accounting and had confiscated his computer, saying that he was suspected of engaging in child pornography. He was not arrested, and as yet, they had heard nothing else. The computer had not been returned.

"I don't know what to believe," Mary Jane said, her voice almost choking. "He says that he has never been involved with child pornography. He has admitted that he has in the past viewed other pornography, but he has stopped."

The pastor was puzzled. Was Kurt guilty? Was Mary Jane overreacting? Throughout all of this, Kurt remained unresponsive. The pastor wondered what it would be like, if one were innocent, to be accused of being a potential child molester to one's pastor. He knew that Kurt had become interested in meditation and had practiced it daily, and now it was almost as if he were in a meditative state. He asked him how he thought this might have happened.

Kurt answered in a flat monotone voice. He said he didn't really know. He knew that he was innocent. He knew that even though the university computers were interconnected, he didn't think it was possible for someone to download something to his computer from another site, even if that person knew his password.

The pastor asked if there was any way for them to get a status of the investigation, to find out if he was still a "person of interest," or if the matter had simply been dropped, and, if so, why had his computer not been returned.

Kurt explained matter-of-factly that they had retained a lawyer, and that he had been advised simply to wait and not to stir the pot. Mary Jane was clearly impatient with that advice. Kurt didn't seem to care one way or the other.

***

Steve was a useful person to have around. He worked in the IT department of a major company and thus was very knowledgeable about computers. Since Pastor Malcolm, a pastor in his sixties, felt like a real klutz when it came to any kind of technology, he was relieved to be able to call on Steve to fix the office equipment when something went wrong or to explain to him what he needed to do in order to get a program to work right.

If people were asked to come up with an adjective to describe Steve, most would come up with the word *quiet.* He was pleasant and appeared likeable, but he never said much. In a group, he had a way of disappearing.

Pastor Malcolm was saddened when he learned that Steve and his wife had filed for divorce. He arranged to meet with them in his study. He learned that she had had an affair. That, however, to his surprise, was not the reason for the divorce. When informed of the affair, Steve had taken it more or less in stride. He indicated that he understood. He forgave her. That, she said, was the last straw. She had tried for years, she said, to establish some kind of emotional connection with him. He was a nice man. She didn't wish him any ill will. But she felt constantly lonely in his presence. She saw no option but to get a divorce.

Pastor Malcolm stared at Steve, wondering what his response would be. He nodded his head in understanding.

General Description

Schizoid Personality Disorder

Schizoids demonstrate a pervasive pattern of detachment from social relationships and appear to have few, if any, close relationships. Their most noticeable trait is indifference, and they seem unable to form close attachments. They feel self-sufficient and have no particular need for friendships. They enjoy solitary activities like reading, computer games, and individual hobbies. They typically have little if any interest in sex. They are often indifferent to both praise and criticism. They appear detached with little emotional expression. They may have difficulty identifying beliefs and values that are important to them.

The situations in which the characteristics of the schizoid become evident are in close personal relationships.

Others often view them as cold or aloof. They lack spontaneity. They sometimes appear distracted and seem inept and awkward in social situations. It is often difficult to enter into a conversation with them, as they share little personal information. They sometimes are regarded as boring. They often can become nearly invisible.

Schizoids often hold an intellectual understanding of God, but it is an understanding that lacks emotional content. Affective experiences of God, including experiencing God as close or nurturing, are often lacking.

In congregational settings, they will seldom call attention to themselves or engage in conversation with anyone. They may sometimes appear to be model parishioners: reliable and faithful, seldom causing problems, but because their needs are often overlooked, are seldom helped or cared for in a meaningful way. Spiritually, they seem to have an intellectual understanding of God, but words like *love* and *joy* and *hope* seem devoid of any emotional content.

Schizoid Personality Style

Individuals with a schizoid style are even-tempered and dispassionate. Though they are most comfortable being alone, they don't mind being in the company of others. They are little driven by needs and are not significantly swayed either by praise or criticism. They are often deep thinkers and analytical about their approach to life.

***

Drama Pattern with Schizoid PD

(Schizoids seldom enter into drama patterns, but they create drama patterns around them, turning rescuers into victims, victims into persecutors, and persecutors into victims.)

In some ways, schizoids are an exception to the drama pattern in the fact that they themselves typically don't participate. Their non-responsiveness, however, can lead the people who attempt interactions with them into noticeable drama patterns.

For example, someone might begin an interaction with a schizoid as a rescuer, feeling that this must be a person who is lonely or depressed, desiring to help. When the schizoid doesn't respond as expected, the rescuer begins to feel like a victim, assuming that he or she must have failed and done something wrong.

Others may believe a schizoid in his or her quiet manner to be a caring person and attempt to enter a relationship in the role of a victim, seeking compassion. When the schizoid doesn't respond, he or she switches into the persecutor role: "What's your problem, anyway?"

Persecutors who become angry with schizoids for their failure to provide any emotional connection sometimes are accused of being heartless for becoming angry with or rejecting "such a nice person."

9 SCHIZOTYPAL PERSONALITY
(CLUSTER A—ODD PARISHIONERS, CHALLENGES TO ASSIMILATION)

Snapshots

Michael worked as a sacker in a local grocery store. He sometimes attempted to engage the customers in conversation, but they always seemed to be in a hurry. Often he would talk to them anyway as he carried out their groceries, but if at first they tried to show interest, they soon stopped responding. Usually it was because they couldn't follow what he was saying. He talked rapidly, skipping quickly from one subject to another with no obvious connection. As soon as the groceries were safely deposited in the trunk of the car, they were ready to be on their way.

In church, Michael always sat by himself—the third pew from the front on the left. When it came time to say the Lord's Prayer or the Apostles Creed, he said it very loudly and very deliberately, forcing everyone else who tended to mumble these words and rush through them to slow down and match his pace.

Pastor Daryl took him under his wing and gave him a lot of attention, joking with him and introducing him to others as "the most devoted member of First Church" and from time to time giving him little jobs to do around the church. He discovered that Michael was a great admirer of Houdini and knew almost everything about his life. He even had a pair of handcuffs and demonstrated to Pastor Daryl his ability to get out of them. Michael responded happily to the attention.

On the pastor's birthday, he bought an elaborate gift with a card saying, "We are the best of friends. I would do anything for you! (You know what I mean!)."

Later, when he saw Pastor Daryl in church, he inquired eagerly if he had gotten the card and gift. He seemed bubbling over with happiness and winked at him before he left.

Pastor Daryl was confused. Had his efforts to include Michael in the community been misconstrued?

***

Allen served as an usher at Christ Community Church. He always wore a Green Bay Packers hat, which, on game days, was turned around backward and a little off kilter in the superstitious belief that they played better when he followed this custom. Members of the congregation who knew him well knew not to ask about the Packers, as he was likely to launch into a detailed account of players, statistics, and history that went back many years. They could even be detained in the church aisle, not allowed to seat themselves until he finished this recitation. A few had on ongoing bet that promised a free dinner at a local restaurant to anyone who asked him something about the Packers that he would not know. Since few wanted to hear him recite endless minutiae, to date, no one had even attempted.

Allen was short, but almost always wore a pair of pants that was even somewhat shorter, ending somewhere above his ankles. He didn't wear socks.

He liked the job of ushering: always arriving early, completing each step of the ushers' duties in precise order, checking lights, checking sound system, checking to make sure the offering plates were in place. Indeed, he was one of those who, if for some reason he missed a Sunday (which was seldom), everything seemed to go awry as few realized all the little details he took care of. He seemed happy. Sometimes one could even hear him emit a little giggle as he walked up and down the aisles, attending to his tasks.

He lived in a house with his mother. His room, as one might expect, was bedecked with all sorts of Green Bay Packers memorabilia. As far was anyone could tell (though few even bothered to inquire), he had no friends.

***

The congregation knew him as the "Green Marshmallow." The tradition apparently began a number of years ago when he had had a small part in a humorous dinner theater drama by that name, which the congregation had staged as a fund raiser. He had basked in the attention it brought him, and he was fond of reminiscing about it. And, true to form, he regularly brought a green marshmallow salad to every congregational pot luck.

Though nearly everyone knew Gene and liked him, it would be difficult to say that anyone was really "friends" with him—other than a sister with whom he seemed quite close and who came to visit twice a year. Whenever anyone tried to talk with him, it was as if they talked past one another rather than engaged in a conversation. The topic of conversation would frequently take unexpected jumps so that one was really never sure what he or she was talking about. He had a habit also of starting phrases that sounded like a familiar proverb, but they never were completed or were twisted in unexpected ways, like: "a fish in time is mine" or "a leopard has spots" or "don't sweat the cooking." He would say these phrases with such an air of finality that it seemed as though, for him at least, the subject under discussion had been magically disposed of, though for others, the subject (whatever it was) had just disappeared into the magician's hat.

***

The Mickelbergs were worried about their son Ethan. After graduating from high school, having no interest in college, he had moved into an apartment and had worked for a couple of months as a forklift operator in a warehouse before quitting to take a part-time job at a fast-food restaurant. After a year, he quit that job also, saying that he hated it, and he moved back home. He stayed up all night, participating in multiplayer computer games. He adopted the name Gondolfo for his online identity. The individuals he played with sometimes texted him. There were online feuds, flirtations, threats, boasts, betrayals, and friendships. He sometimes fantasized that he would go and live with some of these phantom acquaintances, but then there was always that troubling issue of money.

The Mickelbergs seldom saw their son, because in the mornings he tended to sleep in. When they did cross paths, they pressed him about making job applications and writing a resume, and he replied with vague answers. They knew though he hadn't actually gone to any job interviews, because he didn't have a car, and he had never asked to use theirs. Adding to their worry was the fact that Sam Mickelberg had developed bone cancer. Thus, their concern about Ethan's future had become even greater.

Not knowing what else to do, they turned to their pastor, Pastor Sara. Pastor Sara knew Ethan only slightly. While growing up, Ethan had attended church fairly regularly, but since graduating from high school and moving away for a while, he now seldom was there. What she remembered about him was just that he seemed odd—not in a crazy sort of way: just eccentric, not fitting in, somewhat of a loner. She wasn't sure how she could help but agreed to meet with him.

When he arrived at her office, he was wearing shorts (though it was midwinter) and a Mickey Mouse T-shirt. He didn't seem to mind talking to her. But when pressed about what he wanted, what he would like to do with his life, what he saw as his talents, he didn't seem to know. The one thing he was sure about was that he didn't want to work at a fast-food job again.

Not knowing really how to help him, Pastor Sara made a referral to a therapist she knew. When the therapist asked what she thought his abilities or potential were, she replied, "I don't really know. Maybe he won't ever be much different from what he is right now."

General Description

Schizotypal Personality Disorder

Schizotypal individuals exhibit a pervasive pattern of social and interpersonal deficits, including: odd behaviors, cognitive and perceptual distortions, and acute discomfort with close relationships. Their most noticeable trait is their eccentricity. They are nonconformists. They tend to view themselves as special and unique but are wary of others who may be hurtful to them.

They may exhibit odd beliefs and magical thinking and often

have unusual speech patterns. Though generally likeable, others are often puzzled by them. Conversations with them sometimes elicit confusing remarks or unusual ideas, and communication is difficult because of their tendency to jump from one subject to another and their odd nonsequiturs.

They often have unusual beliefs characterized by magical thinking and superstitious behavior. Their perception of self is distorted, and they may see themselves as gifted, insightful, or perceptive. They may also have misperceptions about their body image.

Their affect is limited and sometimes inappropriate as they may fail to recognize social cues.

These individuals are frequently members of congregations, as the accepting climate of congregations provides them with a welcoming environment. However, they most often operate only on the fringes and strike newcomers, who do not know them well, as strange and even a bit frightening. Spiritually, they may hold to nonorthodox beliefs.

Schizotypal Personality Style

Individuals with Schizotypal style are indifferent to social expectations and sometimes given to acting in odd and unusual ways. They are often interested in unconventional subjects that challenge or provide alternative explanations to accepted beliefs. They are usually self-directed and independent and require few close friends.

Drama Pattern with Schizotypal Personality Disorder

Persecutor switching to victim.

The schizotypal individual may enter a relationship eager to talk about his or her "special knowledge" about arcane subjects and about the "way things really work." When this individual is ignored or if people react to his or her oddness, the person will switch.

10 ANTISOCIAL PERSONALITY
(CLUSTER B—DISRUPTIVE PARISHIONERS, CHALLENGES TO MANAGEMENT)

Snapshots

It seemed to her it had all happened very quickly. He was easy to talk to and shared stories about his family, funny stories that made her laugh, and she found herself telling him about her family. He seemed very interested, asking questions about the town where she grew up, her brothers and sisters, her parents, their pets. It seemed only natural that he should move in with her. It ended, however, almost as quickly as it had begun. In the midst of an argument, he simply got his things together and left. Her anger at him, however, didn't reach its peak until her credit card statement came, and she found out that somehow her maximum balance had been raised, and that a large number of items had been charged against it. Only gradually did it dawn on her that he had used the information he had learned about her to answer security questions concerned with her account. Still, she assumed that once the situation was explained, she would not be held responsible for purchases she didn't make. She was wrong. He made them while she was at home asleep. Since she couldn't prove that she hadn't made the purchases (which she might have, if she had been able to show, for instance, that she was at work, not at home, when they were made), she was held responsible.

***

We were standing in a group, but I could feel his eyes reaching toward me, a highly charged axon, wanting to leap across the synaptic gap between us. I turned to look and met his gaze. He smiled a bemused smile. At first I thought that he was maybe around thirty. He wore blue jeans and a loose cotton shirt and had the nonchalance of youth, but lines on his neck and around his eyes hinted at years that were carefully stored away in his wiry body. He had the intensity of a tiger, strolling aimlessly but observing his surroundings with curiosity. He was perhaps an inch or two shorter than I was, but his presence filled space. Later I saw his exercise room off of the family room on the lower level of his home. It could have easily substituted as a workout room in a small college athletic facility. And workouts, I learned, were not confined to the weight room. He biked, he told me, around 120 miles a week.

Having recently taken up cycling and having discovered how some of the bike trails wound their way through scenic parts of the city, I commented about how wonderful they were. "We could do better," he replied.

He was the CEO of a large insurance company where my wife worked, and he was hired on the basis of his past record with the anticipation that he could make their "good" company "great." After a little less than a year, the board of directors fired him when they learned that most of his past record had been falsified.

***

He had a teddy-bearish appearance: short, stubby legs, rotund stomach, his pants anchored high somewhere above his belly button with a tightly cinched belt. His long and bushy mustache bore a resemblance to Teddy Roosevelt, adding to the image. Only his totally bald head hinted at the internal incongruence with this lovable image. "I think of myself as being like Winnie the Pooh, but I guess sometimes I act more like Tigger with a machine gun."

On one occasion, while serving on riot patrol, his buddy next to him was hit in the head with a thrown brick. He went berserk, seriously injuring five or six of the demonstrators. "I didn't kill anybody," he said, somewhat joyfully, "but I imagine it was five or six days before some of them could move about again." He decided then that maybe serving on the police force was not his cup of tea.

***

Shortly after moving into the neighborhood, he attracted a large crowd after renting a lift truck that raised a hot tub over the house and deposited it in the backyard. We were amazed, since he was a renter. Was the owner aware?

Not long after, he tried to sell us on a sidewalk coloring that he assured us was not paint and would not fade. "You can choose any color you want," he encouraged, "even chartreuse." He used it on his own driveway, having chosen a pale-green color. We briefly considered doing the floor of our garage, but then demurred. After a couple of months, we noticed his driveway began to flake.

The city water works people came by to shut off his water. They had difficulty finding the shut-off valve and spent some time working in his front yard. A couple of days later, he stopped by to inform us that his water had been shut off, and he was on his way down to city hall to get things straightened out. We wondered how he had been living a couple of days without water.

We learned (he told us) that he had obtained a patent for a new invention that made tiles even harder than the space shuttles' tiles. We wondered where he was conducting these experiments.

One summer, he failed to mow his grass all summer. The grass grew so tall that it fully concealed his mower that was standing in the backyard. Several neighbors called in complaints to the mayor.

***

Valley View was a country congregation that was swallowed up by the expanding suburbs of a nearby metropolis. For years, content to be a small church where everybody knew everyone else (and were often interrelated) and maintenance expenses consisted mainly of janitorial supplies, they suddenly experienced a membership boom. In a short period of time, they went from one worship service to three, added on an education wing, and hired additional staff. What they didn't realize at first was how much, at the same time, land prices around them had skyrocketed. Thus, by the time they looked at buying additional property for a new worship space and additional parking, prices seemed beyond their reach.

John Ferrier was among the new members who had come with the membership explosion, and he had been elected chairman of the congregation. No one knew exactly what he did—it had something to do with investments—but he had immediately made an impact. Handsome, confident, soft-spoken, likable, and forward looking, he seemed to be the ideal leader for the changing times through which the congregation was going.

And John had a plan. John told the pastor that an anonymous member of the congregation had approached him about selling a parcel of land that was worth somewhere between $1.2 and $2 million dollars, but that he would sell it to the church for a mere $250,000. The church could then sell the land for its full value, gaining enough in the process to have the proceeds it needed for additional expansion. In order to assure his anonymity, John said, the donor had established a separate trust to conduct the sale of the property.

The congregation, of course, didn't have $250,000. It would require taking out a loan. The idea was discussed. Some didn't like the idea, thinking it best that the congregation rely on the traditional method of fund raising—the generous contributions of its members—rather than resorting to land transactions. But the possibility of what could be done with one million dollars for kingdom expansion proved too much to resist. The loan was approved. The check, made out in the name of the trust fund specified by John Ferrier, was given to John to deliver.

Time passed. John assured the pastor that such things took time, as there were legal matters to be resolved. More time passed. John told the increasingly anxious pastor that an additional $30,000 was needed to pay expenses associated with selling the property to a new purchaser. Reluctant to lose the $250,000 they had already invested, the church came up with the additional $30,000.

John chose not to run for president the following year. He became increasingly more difficult to reach. When finally tracked down, he refused to name the anonymous donor or identify the property in question. He became surly and accused the pastor and other members of harassment.

Eventually, the congregation realized that it needed to take the matter to court. They hired a lawyer and filed a suit. John responded by writing a letter, which he sent to all of the neighboring churches of the denomination, accusing the pastor of defaming his character and disobeying the Bible's injunction against taking a brother to court.

As part of the investigation, a warrant was obtained to search his home. John sued the county, alleging an illegal search of his home.

Eventually, it was learned that the trust had been set up at the request of John. A woman, a friend of John's, acted as the trustee and dispersed the funds to John whenever he requested it. Some of it had been used to pay for his son's college tuition, some for purchases from Victoria's Secret, and some at local casinos.

Throughout the trial, John maintained his innocence, claimed ignorance of many of the things of which he was accused, and insisted that because of his confidentiality agreement, he was not allowed to reveal any of the details of the proposed transaction.

He was eventually sent to prison. The church never received the proceeds of the sale or a refund of its $250,000 payment. The pastor said, "I know we are supposed to forgive, and I'm trying to forgive, but it is difficult to forgive someone who insists that he has done nothing wrong."

***

His telephone interview was impressive. All members of the call committee were convinced that he was the ideal candidate for the position of associate pastor.

The senior pastor eagerly welcomed him and was glad to have the extra help. The new associate made a good first impression and soon began building relationships with members of the congregation.

The senior pastor had planned to devote a considerable amount of time to help his new staff member become oriented, but most of those plans eventually fell by the wayside, as the associate seemed at best indifferent to the information and advice he offered. The senior pastor was glad, in a way, that he seemed independent and wouldn't require much supervision.

One of the earliest indications of his independence was his refusal to the suggestion that it might be best for him to continue to rent for a few months before deciding on a permanent residence in order to give himself time to really get to know the community first. The new associate didn't agree. He wanted to settle his family as soon as possible. He asked about obtaining some additional funds from the congregation in order to make a house purchase. The senior pastor replied that the housing allowance was stipulated in the contract, and he didn't think the congregation should be asked to do more than that.

A few weeks later, the associate approached him about the congregation granting him a loan so that he could purchase a house. The senior pastor said that the congregation wasn't in a position to grant loans, but that their denomination sometimes extended loans to pastors for housing needs. He informed him how to obtain this information.

Not long after this conversation, he learned that his associate had decided to have a new home built. This was disconcerting on two fronts: he knew that his associate had limited finances, and the contractor who had agreed to build this house, a member of the congregation, was not always reliable. He was an individual who was likable and congenial and fun to be around, but though he had many big plans, most seemed to go bust before completion. He voiced these concerns to the associate. The associate's response made him feel like he was being paternalistic, so he let the matter drop.

About this time, the senior pastor took a three weeks' vacation. During the time that the church had been understaffed, he had found it difficult to get away, but now seemed like a good time to enjoy some rest and renewal. Soon after his return, he received some disturbing news. While he was gone, the associate had approached the endowment committee of the church for a construction loan in order to build his new home. He explained to them that their denomination, while they provided housing loans to pastors, did not provide construction loans. He told them that once the project was completed, it would be converted into a regular housing loan, and the endowment committee would receive back their funds. The committee unanimously voted to approve the loan.

The senior pastor felt undermined by these events, but he didn't seem to have any good options. The decision had already been made and couldn't be changed. If he confronted the associate about it now, he reasoned, most likely their working relationship would deteriorate and only make matters worse. If he confronted the members of the endowment committee, who obviously liked their new associate, he feared that he would come across as the one who was creating disharmony on the staff. He decided to do nothing and hope for the best.

Several weeks later, the pastor received a call at church from a man in another state who was stridently demanding that a certain outstanding bill be paid. It eventually became clear that the bill in question was owed by the associate pastor. He informed the individual that the congregation wasn't responsible for his debts, and that he should contact him directly.

Then came a visit from the contractor. He sidled into the office one afternoon and said, "I don't want to get into the middle of this, but there is something that I think you should know." He went on to explain that the construction funds had run out before the completion of the project. He suspected some of it had been misspent. It became clear that the pastor could avoid this problem no longer.

Matters pretty much went downhill after that. He took the matter to the church council, who requested an accounting of the funds from the associate. Numerous delays ensued when excuses were offered, timelines not kept, and incomplete or inaccurate information proffered. It never was possible to determine an exact figure of the misspent funds, but it was clear that a sizable amount had gone for personal items. Sometimes the exchanges between the associate and individuals of the congregation grew heated, degenerating into shouting, name calling, and swear words.

Meanwhile, the associate began to complain to other pastors in the area about the way he was being mistreated and falsely accused. Since he could be quite convincing, the senior pastor found himself in the position of having to defend himself without sounding as if he was being vindictive against his associate.

Eventually, the congregation voted to discontinue the position of associate pastor. On his last official Sunday at church, the associate made a show of wiping the dust off his shoes as he made the way down the aisle for the last time.

***

General Description

Antisocial Personality Disorder

The word "confidence man" was popularized in an 1849 *New York Herald* article detailing the arrest of William Thompson, a man of "genteel appearance," who, for months, had been approaching strangers on the street and somehow persuading them to trust him with their watches until the next day. "Confidence" is an apt description for individuals with antisocial personality disorder. They often appear at first to be confident individuals—charming and sincere. Indeed, they often appear to lack any self-doubt or remorse or moral restraint that might constrain the actions of most people. And they often trade on trust, "confidentially" letting you in on secrets as a step to getting something from you. They are peddlers of hope—and often aren't confronted for their actions, because people keep hoping they are for real.

Individuals with antisocial personality disorder show a pervasive pattern of disregard for the rights of others. They frequently fail to conform to social norms regarding lawful behavior. Their most noticeable trait is exploitation. Their greatest deficiency is honor: they are agreement violators.

If, however, you were able to probe beyond the exterior, you would often find a long history of broken commitments and promises, including a poor work record and failures to honor financial obligations. They often exhibit reckless behavior, showing little regard for their own safety or the safety of others, such as driving while intoxicated or having repeated speeding offenses. They are impulsive, often acting on a whim without a clear goal or plan in mind. They are experts at deceit and weave such a tangle of lies that it is often difficult to ever find out the truth. When confronted with their misdeeds, they are apt to justify their conduct by claiming that they are no different from most people, and attribute to others their own mistrustful, hostile, and vengeful attitudes. In some cases, their aggressive behavior has led to actual physical confrontations. They are not likely to show remorse and appear indifferent when confronted with the way they may have hurt or mistreated others.

The triggering event most likely to reveal the characteristics of an antisocial personality is the discovery of a situation in which the individual refused to conform to social standards or norms.

Individuals with this personality disorder seldom exhibit any feelings such as warmth and intimacy, as these are regarded as signs of weakness.

Their behavior frequently includes the justification that wanting something justifies one's actions. Desire makes right. The views of others or the possibility of consequences have little influence on their decision making.

The spiritual issue for antisocials is a lack of guilt. The construct of "repentance/forgiveness" does not resonate with them emotionally other than as a way to sometimes manipulate people and get out of scrapes. In congregations, they will often take advantage of a trusting atmosphere to engage in illegal activities, often for financial gain. A number of situations relating to embezzlement in congregations have involved individuals with antisocial personality disorder.

Antisocial Personality Style

Individuals with antisocial personality style are strongly independent, quick thinkers, and adept at getting out of difficult situations by using their wits and ingenuity. They tend to live by their own internal code of values and are little influenced by the expectations of others or by sociocultural norms. They are gifted in the art of winning friends and influencing others but tend not to worry too much about others, expecting them to be responsible for themselves. Though they are able to make plans and commitments for limited time spans, for the most part, they tend to live in the present. They like new challenges as they quickly become bored with routine.

Drama Pattern for the Antisocial PD

Rescuer switching to victim or rescuer switching to persecutor.

The antisocial individual enters the drama in the role of a person who is able and willing to fix a problem or provide help: "You can trust me. I promise. You'll thank me a hundred times over when this is done." After these individuals have been caught in their deception or illegal behavior, they switch into the role of someone who has been wronged, pleading for sympathy: "Can't you make an exception just this once?" or "It's not my fault. Can't you see I had to do this?" Or, they may also switch to the role of an accuser, making threats and accusations to keep from being discovered.

11 BORDERLINE PERSONALITY
(CLUSTER B—DISRUPTIVE PARISHIONERS, CHALLENGES TO MANAGEMENT)

Snapshots

In a congregation starving for new members, especially young adults with children, Samantha seemed like a gift from heaven. From the start, Samantha made it known that she had never attended a congregation that was more friendly and welcoming than Westside Baptist Church. And she was quick to let Pastor John know that she absolutely loved his sermons. They were so meaningful to her that she often made notes that she stuck in various places around her house so she could think about it all week long.

Before long, she was involved in many activities at church. Everyone seemed to like her. She was enthusiastic and often funny. She was like a breath of fresh air to their graying congregation that had been for a number of years in a steady decline. She jumped eagerly into a number of church activities.

Samantha attended church with her three children, ages five to nine. Her husband never attended with her. She told others that her husband, in fact, didn't approve of her going to church and tried to prevent her, but she showed up faithfully for every service, increasing the congregation's admiration of her.

After several months, she made an appointment to meet with Pastor John in the church office. She talked about her marriage, about how controlling and sadistic her husband was. Pastor John listened carefully, offered a few suggestions, and said a prayer with her. He wasn't really sure he had been any real help to her, but before long, it came back to him how she was telling nearly everyone about how kind and caring he was and how much help he had been to her. He told himself that if indeed she had been helped, it must have been the work of the Spirit, but he couldn't help but feel be a bit flattered.

But then came the phone calls. At first it was only when he was in the church office. Sometimes she would be in tears, barely able to talk. At others, she said she just wanted to thank him for being so sensitive and supporting. She said, "Never have I met a pastor as caring and sensitive as you. At other churches I have attended, I was never understood and often mistreated." These made him feel good about himself. He felt as if he was helping her, and, her vocal appreciation for his efforts, since he often seemed to hear only criticisms from his members, was like a soothing balm to an open sore. Later, however, the phone calls came at his home, sometimes late at night. Once, she talked about being so miserable she was going to kill herself. He didn't like that these calls came at home, but they did indeed seem to be crisis calls, and he felt good about his ability to talk her out of the abyss of despair. Still, he felt he ought to establish clearer boundaries with her.

Several months after Samantha first became involved at Westside, a single, seventeen-year-old girl who was pregnant also began attending. Pastor John became involved in counseling and lending support to her.

The calls from Samantha abruptly stopped, and soon Pastor John began to hear from some of the ladies of the Bible class that Samantha attended that she was making comments about him to the effect that he was the worst pastor she had ever known, that he was all wrapped up in himself, and could care less about anybody else. Some members were apparently moved by her complaints and sympathized with her.

Pastor John decided that he needed to talk to Samantha and telephoned her. She immediately launched into a tirade, accusing him of misunderstanding and mistreating her (the same accusations she had made against former pastors). "Why are you so selfishly rejecting me?" she wanted to know. It took a while to discover that apparently the event that had set her off was the day she had dropped by the church office to see him, and he was involved with counseling the seventeen-year-old girl. She accused this newcomer of being "manipulative and demanding." As the conversation escalated, he found himself telling her that she was being unreasonable and selfish. She hung up the phone. He immediately regretted losing his temper and figured that he would never see her in church again.

He was wrong. She and her children were there in their usual place the next Sunday. He dreaded the moment that he would have to shake hands with her at the door, but she was cordial and friendly. However, as he soon discovered, the storm she had started within the congregation had not abated but was only growing in strength. Some members who had heard her complaints agreed with her and told their own stories of being ignored or neglected by their pastor. Others, however, recognized inconsistencies in Samantha's stories and viewed her as a troublemaker. One member confronted her and told her that she had an "unforgiving spirit." She immediately flew into a rage. "How dare you question my Christianity," she shouted as she yelled at him, throwing some curse words into the mix. She picked up a chair and was threatening to hit him with it before several others physically restrained her.

A meeting with a number of church leaders was held to discuss the incident. Some felt that a court order banning her from the church premises was necessary. Others felt that was too strong and "unchristian." It was decided that one of them should meet with her to discuss their concerns and to urge her to learn to control her behavior.

Samantha took this as both a rejection and a challenge. She continued attending every service. Sometimes, she would interrupt the worship service, angrily denouncing the pastor and the congregation. "How can God bless hypocrites who don't know how to forgive and love?" she demanded.

For his part, Pastor John worried about her children and what effect all of this was having on them, and he wondered what he had done wrong that led to this tangled mess that was destroying his congregation.

***

Eloisa was in counseling following a failed suicide attempt. Her counselor had recommended that perhaps getting involved in a local congregation could help ease some of the isolation that she often felt. She started attending a large megachurch. She enjoyed the upbeat music and eventually joined a small group Bible study. She liked the ladies who attended this group and became almost instant friends with them. They welcomed her warmly and told her often how glad they were that she was a part of their group.

One Sunday, the subject of the Bible study was regret. The study guide asked that participants share a regret they had experienced within the last week. After a period of silence, one member chipped in that one night she discovered there were still two pieces of cake left, and about an hour later there were none. She wasn't quite sure how that happened! The group laughed knowingly. Another member described how she had gotten into an argument with her husband because he left his dirty socks lying on the floor, and she had realized afterward that there were probably better ways of handling that than calling him a dirty pig. Again, laughter. Eloise began to describe how last night she was feeling unsafe. She didn't know how she could keep going. She wanted to end her life, and in her mind she kept seeing pictures of herself with a rope around her neck, hanging from the ceiling light in the bedroom. So, to get the images to stop, she took a pair of scissors and began to draw lines on her forearms until the blood started to appear and eventually began to create quite a mess. She said she knew she shouldn't do it, but somehow it always seemed to help. Feeling physical pain seemed to make the mental pain go away or at least become less.

The group was silent.

Afterward, several members of the group talked to the staff member who was in charge of small groups, asking her opinion about what to do. The staff member arranged a time to meet with Eloisa. She tried to show compassion and understanding but suggested that maybe she was not the best fit for that group.

Eloisa stopped attending.

***

(See also a description of a borderline personality disorder individual in the opening chapter.)

General Description Borderline of Personality Disorder

The relationship with an individual with borderline personality disorder is like a ride on a roller coaster. One never complains of boredom. Borderlines typically develop very intense relationships with others, but switch rapidly back and forth from expressing admiration and being generous to venting anger and acting punitively. The title of a book about borderlines, *I Hate You—Don't*

Leave Me, expresses this confusing alteration of moods well.

The situation most likely to trigger the characteristics of a borderline personality is any in which the individual begins to experience either real or imagined abandonment.

The source of their unpredictable moods and lack of consistency appears to be an unstable self-image. Unsure of their true nature, they either see themselves as vulnerable and others as rejecting and hostile or themselves as admirable and others as appreciative and worshipful. Others thus become either "angels" or "devils," seldom anything between. They are very adept at self-justification, quite certain in their convictions that their intense like or dislike of others is fully justified. At the same time, they may frequently change their own attitude about career goals, types of friends, or important values.

When not sustained by intense relationships, they have chronic feelings of deep emptiness and loneliness and will go to almost any length to avoid either real or imagined abandonment. This leads to impulsive behavior, which frequently manifests itself with problems in regards to spending, sexual behavior, reckless driving, shoplifting, or binge eating. They may exhibit suicidal or self-injury behaviors. They often experience sleep disorders and may go through long periods without sleep or endure sleep that is frequently interrupted by nightmares.

Some are initially enamored by borderlines. Others feel sorry for them and make excuses for them, only later to become angry and confused, feeling that no matter what they do or don't do, they are accused of having let them down. They will seem sometimes dependent and at other times hostile. Their demands often are unreasonable, and relationships with them will often be stormy. They will seldom apologize.

The faith issue for those with borderline personality disorder is the reliability of God. The same switching between adoration and antagonism that borderlines exhibit in their personal relationships can frequently also be evident in their faith relationship with God.

General Description of Borderline Personality Style

These individuals tend to be quite emotional and put their feelings and heart into everything. Their relationships are apt to be quite passionate, and nothing in their relationships, either its positive aspects or its difficulties, is taken lightly. They frequently are fun loving and spontaneous. They can be very creative and engaging individuals. They are curious and enjoy exploring new things. They are often deeply involved in a romantic relationship with one individual.

Drama Pattern for Borderline Personality Disorder

Victim changing to persecutor or rescuer changing to persecutor.

They initially will attempt to establish a relationship either as one who has been failed or hurt by others ("See how others are mistreating me?") or as a caring helper ("You've really gotten the short end of the stick. Let me be your best friend."). Very quickly, however, the role will switch to that of an angry critic ("You are a bad person for not being available to me!").

12 HISTRIONIC PERSONALITY (CLUSTER B—DISRUPTIVE PARISHIONERS, CHALLENGES TO MANAGEMENT)

Snapshots

Jack was a deeply devoted pastor, desiring to minister effectively to his parishioners. After the last service, Jack was comfortably ensconced in his office preparing for a meeting that evening when Nancy, a single woman and a parishioner for some years, appeared at the door. She asked if she could come in. During the four months of Jack's pastorate at that congregation, he had developed a casual relationship with Nancy. She was difficult not to notice in a crowd—blond, trim, always neatly dressed, and fashionably attired. He knew that she had been through a series of relationships with men, which appeared to have ended badly. Sometimes she would joke with him in a flirtatious sort of way, which he reciprocated in kind, thinking it was her way of rising above the sadness in her life. He certainly didn't take it seriously, as he was a married man.

When Nancy entered the office, she closed the door behind her and moved closer to Jack's desk. As was his custom, Jack stood and began to walk around the desk to greet her. On this day, however, he stopped at the edge of the desk.

After a moment's hesitation, Nancy blurted out that she found Jack attractive and wanted to "make love" to him. Jack was initially shocked into speechlessness but quickly found himself saying, "I can't believe you would dare say this to me. I am a pastor. You need to leave immediately!"

The woman looked stunned. Tears welled up in her eyes, and she left the office sobbing. Jack sensed that he had done something wrong but was unsure what he could have or should have done differently.

***

When Russ became senior pastor of Bethany Lutheran Church, he knew that one of his first tasks was to assess the current staff. When he asked one of the other staff members about Belinda, inquiring, "What does she do?" he was told, "Drama." When he raised an eyebrow wondering whether or not he was serious, the response was, "That's it. She creates drama. She's the dependable source of the 'crisis de jour.'"

In actuality, Belinda was in charge of the children's ministry. She was tall and slender. At one time she had been a dancer. She was outgoing and bubbly and tended to dress flamboyantly. Children liked her and were drawn to her. She was like a cartoon character.

But it wasn't long before Pastor Russ discovered that the characterization of her role that he had been given was not far from the truth. Nearly every week some conflict seemed to arise, either instigated by her or directed at her.

Shortly after his arrival, he had informed the staff that we would meet individually with each of them to discuss their ministry and to lay out in some detail his expectations. Belinda was the only one who resisted. She took every one of his expectations as a form of criticism. She said repeatedly, "I don't see why you are being so mean; everybody likes me!"

One of her responsibilities was to lead a children's message on Sunday mornings. These she did with great flair, using many gestures, but often they seemed to be only tangentially related to the biblical text she was supposed to talk about and more about herself than a message about faith. Once, to illustrate the story of the prayers of the Pharisee and tax collector in the temple, she had the children sing the "Itsy Bitsy Spider" song and went on to describe the many disappointments she had faced in life (once she thought she had lost her car keys but found them stuck down between the cushions of her couch). "However," she emphasized, "you should never get down on yourself, because sooner or later the sun will come out again!"

Inevitably, she didn't live up to the expectations on her job description. The pastor called her into his office and informed her that it was necessary to let her go.

The following Sunday, he made the announcement to the congregation. He was a bit surprised that she showed up at church that Sunday. In the announcement, he attempted to describe her past work at Bethany in the most affirming way possible, mentioning her years of service and her accomplishments. He gave as the reason for her departure the vague: "It is time for Bethany to explore some new directions with the design and makeup of our staff to meet the challenges of the changing nature of our community." At the conclusion of the announcement, Belinda got up and began to dance her way to the exit with ballerina-like gestures, singing as she went "Good-bye. So long. I guess you don't like me anymore. It's been so good to know you."

***

Dennis at one time had a notable tenor voice. Over the years, he had developed a reputation as a soloist at funerals. Actually, though, his preference was for singing at church, for often at the conclusion of his solo, there was applause. He confided to his pastor that he didn't really enjoy singing for funerals that much because people weren't allowed to clap. Those Sundays when he sang, his entire pew was filled as all of his family came. The Sundays he didn't sing, none of them were there.

The crisis came when the choir director suggested that due to his aging, he was perhaps more of a baritone than a tenor. He was deeply offended and quit both the choir and the congregation. He continued to serve as a funeral soloist and was often requested. He tried to imagine that even the deceased would applaud if only it were permissible.

***

June and Birdie both lived in a federally subsidized retirement home for seniors. June was envious of Birdie because Birdie seemed to have a knack for gaining attention. Moving slowly with her walker she found ways to create somewhat of a traffic jam, which led to many people stopping to talk to her. She loved to tell the story that had earned the nickname "Birdie": when she was born she fit into a shoe box, and her father had said, "Why she ain't no bigger than a bird!" And the nickname had stuck.

Meanwhile, while Birdie reiterated this story for the umpteenth time, June stood nearby, silently seething, as she had to wait for her in order to ride with her back to their apartments.

June had never married, but it was clear from photos in her apartment that she had once been somewhat of a "looker." And even now, she had devised her way of getting attention.

Once every year she entered the hospital. Her pastor came to visit. She was in the prayers at church. A few people sent cards. A variety of tests were run. Nothing was ever found. She stayed as long as Medicaid allowed and was always relieved to find that she was okay. Unfortunately, another year would pass before Mecaid would pay for another opportunity to receive the attention she desired.

***

Soon after her arrival, Jaylon took Pastor Grace aside and assured her, "I've got your back. If I hear any bad talk about you, I'll see that it is squelched at once."

Pastor Grace wasn't exactly encouraged by this assurance. She wondered what the past history of this congregation was that pastors needed their own security detail. What kind of protection was Jaylon offering? She told another pastor friend, "Sometimes when he is around, it seems that I'm hearing behind me the noise of a blade being sharpened on a grindstone."

She soon discovered that Jaylon fished the gossip circles for impending crises. Whenever he caught wind of something, he was in on it, making sure everyone knew he was coming to the rescue, giving advice, plotting "battle plans," engaging in confrontation. He was Sir Galahad, Rin Tin Tin, and the Lone Ranger all rolled into one. He lived life as if he were Indiana Jones and the world a place of endless adventures.

General Description

Histrionic Personality Disorder

A person with histrionic personality disorder is characterized by a pervasive pattern of excessive emotionality and attention-seeking behavior. These individuals like to be the center of attention. They exaggerate a great deal and overdramatize whatever they are describing. They overreact, either with excessive delight or excessive complaints, in a way that is out of proportion to whatever has occurred.

The triggering event that displays the characteristics of histrionic personality may involve opposite-sex relationships, though any situation in which the individual feels that he or she is receiving insufficient attention may elicit the traits.

They tend to believe that they must be loved by everyone in order to be okay, and they seek to gain that approval by "performing." Often, the assumption seems to be that if they are not adored and worshiped by everyone, then they have failed and are rejected by all.

Great attention is given to externals, to appearance, and to actions that provide opportunities to draw attention to them. They often dress seductively or engage in flirtatious behavior. They can be both charming and inconsiderate, expressive and demanding. They often think their relationships with others are more intimate than they really are. They frequently enter sexual relationships by acting as a willing but submissive partner, assuming that a show of dependency is the best way to attract and control the opposite sex.

Even criticism or disapproval can be a way of getting attention, and though they don't like it, they sense that it is better than being ignored. Exaggerated emotional displays and temper tantrums are not uncommon.

Histrionics often have a history of difficult-to-diagnose physical complaints, which appear to be another way to be noticed. They know that after being caught in an embarrassing or humiliating situation, it can also be useful for redirecting criticism into sympathy.

Conversations with them tend to be vague, lacking in specifics. They will sometimes throw tantrums or display fits of temper to get their way. This may also include suicide threats or attempts.

They are often very expressive but lack a sense of shame. They see themselves as fetching and all others as potential admirers. All the world, to them, is a stage.

Others tend to see them as needy and overly emotional. Though friendships develop quickly with them, they often soon become inconsiderate, egocentric, deceitful, and demanding. Their constant demand for attention and their vague and dramatic exaggerations become exasperating.

Faith is a difficult concept for them, as they feel driven to get the affirmation they need. The idea that it is already there and doesn't need to be provoked doesn't fit with their expectations or life experiences.

Histrionic Personality Style

Individuals with a histrionic style enjoy compliments and praise, but they don't have an excessive need for them. They like being the center of attention and generally perform better when they have such recognition. They give attention to their appearance and like clothes, fashion, and style. They are lively, fun loving, and creative, and they are physically affectionate. They are aware of the influence their behavior and appearance may have on other people but generally do not use this influence inappropriately.

Drama Pattern for the Histrionic PD

Victim changing to persecutor changing changing back to victim.

Histrionics typically enter a relationship in drama in a helpless manner, putting themselves down in some way ("Don't you feel sorry for me?" "Surely you don't think I could be the cause of such a ruckus!"). They switch into a critical role ("Look at me! I'm special! Don't you find me attractive?"). And when others withdraw attention, they switch back into a victim ("You really don't care! You are such an awful person!").

13 NARCISSISTIC PERSONALITY
(CLUSTER B—DISRUPTIVE PARISHIONERS, CHALLENGES TO MANAGEMENT)

Snapshots

"Pastor, I need to talk to you. I've been reading this amazing book, and I'm eager to tell you all about it."

There was a time when Pastor Warren felt pleased when Jill called, saying she wanted to meet with him. Here at last was someone actually seeking his advice. It fulfilled his need to be needed. But after several repetitions of this, he began to be annoyed. He wasn't sure exactly what she wanted, but it had become clear it wasn't advice.

"I'm really only going to be here for a few more minutes. I'm on my way to make hospital calls."

"It's a book by M____. She's a Christian psychologist. I only read books by Christian authors, as you know. It's the most amazing book. She's told me things about myself that I never knew. She said that each of us has the voice of God within us, and that we just need to listen to that voice. And I think that is just what I've been doing all along, and I just never realized it! You know, when I went through my divorce with Mark, he tried to make me feel like it was all my fault, that I was totally wrapped up in myself, and that I was just using him but never really cared about what he was thinking or feeling, and I knew, I just knew, that wasn't true. That was the voice of God telling me that I was right! And when I had to fire Janet at work because she just wasn't doing her job—I had told her a hundred times to use the color copier to print the reports, but she kept saying she was saving money, not realizing what that looked like to everyone else—she cried and carried on, but I knew it was the right thing to do, and I think that was the voice of God as well."

"We have lots of voices in us. How do you know which one is God's voice?"

"What do you mean?"

"Well, I'm not saying you actually hear 'voices,' but there are always all kinds of thoughts running through our minds. Sometimes it is self-doubt; sometimes it is wishful thinking; sometimes it is the voice of temptation. How do you know which is God's voice?"

"Well, I think it's pretty clear. I never have any trouble knowing."

"Hmm. Well, I suppose that means you must be well grounded in God's Word."

"What do you mean?"

"God speaks to us primarily through his Word. If we want to be attuned to his voice, we have to first learn to listen and take in what he says."

"But that's why I wanted to meet with you. You know his Word and have always been very affirming to me."

For a brief moment, Pastor Warren understood why it was that though Jill seemed to frequently come to him for advice, she never seemed interested in receiving any. "I don't believe I've ever seen you attend any of the Bible studies at church."

"I'm sure they're very good, but you know how busy I've been. I just can't fit them into my schedule. But I'm glad when I get a chance to talk to you. It helps keep me on the right track."

Resistance melted with the compliment. He agreed to make an appointment with her on the following day, though he had the feeling it would mostly be an opportunity for her to talk about all of the things she had been doing lately.

***

The opening of the worship service was a little like the opening monologue of the *Tonight Show*. After welcoming everyone and giving them an update on the fund-raising campaign to purchase new audio visual equipment for the sanctuary, sometimes stopping

midsentence to call out someone by name whom he recognized—
"Oh, Mary, how's that baby boy? Is he still keeping you up nights?"
"Hi there, Jessica. Glad to see you back. Feeling better now?"—he
launched into a story:

> There was this Baptist preacher who decided
> to get a new dog. But he didn't want just any dog,
> no sinful bark-and-everything kind of dog. He
> wanted a Baptist dog. At the dog kennel, he made
> the request. The kennel operator didn't flinch for a
> moment.
>
> "We have exactly what you want. We have a
> genuine, dyed in the wool, Baptist dog."
>
> "How do you know he's a Baptist dog?" the
> skeptical preacher asked.
>
> "Watch," said the kennel owner. "Fetch the
> Bible," he commanded. The dog bounded to the
> bookshelf, scrutinized the books, located the Bible,
> and brought it to the owner.
>
> The preacher was impressed. But the kennel
> owner wasn't finished.
>
> "Now find Psalm 23," he commanded. The
> dog dropped the Bible to the floor and showing
> marvelous dexterity with his paws, leafed through
> and, finding the correct passage, pointed to it with
> his paw.
>
> The preacher was amazed and purchased the
> dog. He couldn't wait to show him off to members
> of his congregation. At church that evening, he put
> him through his paces and had him locate several
> Bible verses. The congregation was quite in awe.
>
> But one man asked, "Can he do regular dog
> tricks, too?"
>
> "I haven't tried yet," the pastor replied. He
> pointed his finger at the dog. "Heel!" the pastor
> commanded. The dog jumped up on the pulpit and
> placed one paw on the pastor's forehead and began
> to howl.
>
> "My Lord," said the man. "That ain't no Baptist
> dog. He's a Pentecostal."

The congregation had a good laugh, but some were beginning to become uneasy. That routine at the beginning of the service went on nearly every Sunday. Some were starting to feel that their pastor was more interested in calling attention to himself than in leading people to worship God.

He had seemed the ideal candidate when he was interviewed. In a very casual way, he described the previous successes he had had in ministry. It was quite impressive. And, in some ways, since his arrival, he had lived up to expectations. He was outgoing and likeable. He had a knack for recognizing the people with money, built relationships with them, and had been very successful in fundraising. He had added staff.

Yet, problems had begun to appear. New staff didn't always stay very long, and often it was the ones who appeared to be the most successful and the most liked by the congregation who didn't last. It was reported that one of them had had a mental breakdown after a confrontation with him. It was almost as if he liked the idea of a large staff because it showed that he was a successful senior pastor, but he didn't like successful members on his staff, because it took attention away from him.

There were also reports of questionable and possibly illegal behavior. The financial secretary told a member of the church council that in the midst of a fund-raising project for a building expansion, the pastor told her to misreport the figures in the bulletin, putting in a lower figure than that actually received, in order to encourage more giving.

Staff relationships continued to deteriorate, and a church consultant was contacted to work separately with staff to get to the bottom of the issue. The consultant had every member of the staff complete two personality inventories, answering once for themselves, and one as they believed it applied to the senior pastor. The senior pastor was also asked to complete the inventory for himself. The staff's portrait of the senior pastor was virtually unanimous in its depiction. They saw him as very driven, goal oriented, but lacking empathy. The senior pastor's self-report indicated that he saw himself as empathetic, loyal, compassionate, team oriented. When the consultant met separately with the senior pastor to discuss this discrepancy, he expressed surprise and wanted to talk about other individuals who, he said, saw him as empathetic and kind. The consultant learned, though, that the pastor had two adult children. One had changed his name and had moved to another part of the country, and the pastor hadn't had any contact with him in over three years. The other was in a mental institution after attempting suicide.

The impasse with the staff unresolved, the pastor took a call to another state, where, it was feared, the same process would reoccur.

***

General Description

Narcissistic Personality Disorder

Individuals with narcissistic personality disorder are preoccupied with self-image. Unlike histrionics who seek to fuel an inner emptiness by gaining attention from others, narcissists want or need little from others other than that which feeds their self-aggrandizement. They are full of big ideas, which they are gifted at describing in glowing terms but that, upon closer examination, often are lacking in specific details. They exude self-confidence and have an aura of nonchalance about them—until their confidence is shaken, when they are likely to respond with rage. Thus, the triggering event that often brings forth the features of a narcissistic personality is likely to be a situation in which their self-image experiences a setback.

Narcissists lack empathy and have little interest or understanding about the feelings of others. They are often interpersonally exploitative, utilizing shame and verbal abuse either to get their way or to punish those who appear to detract from their image. At the same time, they are envious of those they deem successful, and they like to associate with those they perceive to be exceptionally talented, wise, or gifted.

They have a grandiose sense of self-importance. They perceive themselves as different from others in significant ways and tend to disregard any information that appears contradictory to that belief. They are masters of exaggeration and seldom reveal anything about themselves that reveals weakness or failure. A capacity for self-evaluation and self-criticism seems to be absent. They believe others are envious of them. Their excessive demand for admiration is seldom satisfied.

They have a sense of entitlement that believes rules don't necessarily apply to them. They may freely disregard the rights of others while assuming or demanding special favors.

They think of themselves as special and others exist to fulfill their needs. They deal with the world by image management.

Contrary to what is sometimes thought, they are not so much in love with self as in love with their image. Though they appear egocentric, they frequently are insecure and use image management as a defense mechanism. Personal attacks can either lead to vindictive counterattacks, or, when there appears to be no escape, they may quite literally "go to pieces." In a fragile state, they resort to excessive apologies and contrite behavior in an attempt to restore their image.

Often people at first are impressed by them and their evident confidence and record of success. After a period of time, however, many come to regard them as uncaring, arrogant, and insensitive. Some try to placate or please them. Others are irritated by them, avoid them, and may end up hating them.

There is some evidence that narcissism is on the increase. Jean Twnege and Keith Campell, in *The Narcissism Epidemic*, argue that the incidence of narcissistic personality disorder has more than doubled in the United States in the last ten years. Recently, a group of researchers conducted a computer analysis of three decades of hit songs. The researchers reported a statistically significant trend toward narcissism and hostility in popular music. In line with their hypothesis, they found a decrease in usages of words such as *we* and *us* and an increase in *I* and *me*.

According to St. Augustine, hubris, or man *curvatus in se* (turned in upon himself), is the fundamental sin and the source of all others.

It is difficult for narcissists to recognize the need for God other than as a means to inflate their own sense of self-importance. Yet, because of their apparent confidence and self-assuredness, in congregational settings these individuals often assume the role of congregational leaders or clergy, but there is, however, often shallowness about their endeavors, as if God is being used rather than being served.

Narcissistic Personality Style

Individuals with narcissistic personality style enjoy challenges and love getting to the top and staying there. They are capable leaders and use the talents (and sometimes the weaknesses) of others to accomplish their goals. They are adept at promoting their ideas and their projects to others. They have confidence in their abilities and do not need a great deal of praise, and they do not demand special treatment or privileges. They are sensitive to the criticisms of others, but they have learned over a period of time how to handle negative assessments with style and grace.

Drama Pattern for Narcissistic Personality Disorders

Rescuer switching to persecutor.

Individuals with narcissistic personality disorder enter the drama as heroes and saviors ("I have special skills and abilities. I know just what you need."). When rebuffed, they quickly become critical and aggressive, exhibiting considerable anger ("You have really let me down." "You are totally incompetent.").

14 AVOIDANT PERSONALITY
(CLUSTER C—ANXIOUS PARISHIONERS, CHALLENGES TO MEANINGFUL CARE)

Snapshots

A nearby church camp for youth was in need of a "people mover," a vehicle that could transport individuals to different areas of its extensive natural habitat. The congregation was sympathetic. They valued the camp ministry and liked the idea of doing something for those who would be the "future church." However, they had their own financial problems. After much discussion, they voted to make a donation of two hundred dollars, far short of what was needed.

Sometime later, Pastor Jill learned that members of her congregation, Bill and Diana, had donated the remainder of the funds that were needed, and the camp had its new "people mover." "That's just like them," she thought. They had always been quite friendly to her, but as far as she could tell, they had few close relationships in the congregation. Bill had short silvery hair and always talked fast as if he was in a hurry to leave and needed to get the words out before his body departed. Diana smiled a lot and said little. They sat in the back of the church and after services exited out a side door of the church. But Jill knew that though they were always reluctant to get involved in any way, when it came down to it, they were the ones who could be counted on to show care in some way, though often anonymously.

***

Mark was the chair of evangelism committee of the congregation, a role that seemed to fit him well, as he had served for twenty years selling insurance. But when the suggestion was made that the evangelism committee do follow-up calls on those who visited the congregation, Mark abruptly resigned. When asked why, he indicated that was something he felt he could not do. The very idea absolutely paralyzed him.

"But wasn't that something you did when selling insurance?" he was asked.

"No," he insisted. "I never made any cold calls. I never want to go any place where I am not invited or where people might wonder, 'what are you doing here?'"

Putting two and two together, the pastor began to understand why Mark had also always resisted the idea of setting "stretch goals"—goals that seemed just a bit beyond one's reach. The idea of not meeting a goal was anathema to him, and he couldn't understand why the church would ever want to make its members feel that way.

Since evangelism wasn't his place, other options were considered. It was finally suggested that he might serve as the coffee host on Sunday morning. This turned out to be a good fit. He faithfully showed up every Sunday. The coffee was always ready on time. Afterward, all the dishes were washed and the trash put away. As people came to get their coffee, people seldom saw him, but that didn't seem to matter. Mark was delighted to be able to serve in this invisible way.

***

His brow would furrow as he looked at me over the tops of his glasses. He was partially bald, with a mustache, of slim build, but with his shirt open at the collar, revealing a hairy (slightly graying) chest. He reminded me of the way a mild ticket taker or conductor would be portrayed in a Walt Disney cartoon.

He was the oldest of three brothers. His father was a fireman. They lived in Washington, and in the summertime, he would take them to the beach to look for seashells. His father walked ahead of them as they hunted for the treasures. Only later did they begin to realize that the shells they found had been dropped by him—they were shells from the South Pacific.

From an early age, he remembers his parents fighting. It distressed him greatly. By the time he was six, he assumed the responsibility of taking care of his two younger brothers, while his parents fought. Around six or seven, his parents divorced.

After the divorce, he changed school many times. He learned to isolate. His mom was remarried to a man who lived on a farm and had little interest in books or reading.

His mom drank heavily, and on the weekends, often his stepdad's younger brother would take care of them. He was a pedophile. Thus, from ages twelve to fourteen, he was frequently sexually abused. He told no one. He developed an interest in boy scouts as a way of getting away from home.

In his early teens, he finally told his dad about what had happen. His dad called a meeting with his ex-wife and her husband and asked them about it. The meeting did not go well. In the end, his father sent him back to live with his mom. He said, "I can't do anything. She has custody." The weekend after he was back home, he was sent to his grandparents, who sat him on a chair and grilled him all day, trying to get him to admit that his dad had put him up to making the accusations. He refused to answer any of their questions, though they took turns going at him for hours.

After telling his cousin what had happened, his cousin spread the story around school, which caused him untold grief and led to further isolation.

Sometime later, his mother attempted suicide. Though she survived, he ended up back living with his father, who had remarried, and he and his second wife were concerned about his social isolation and the time he spent in his room. They encouraged him to get involved in school activities. He chose long-distance running and the chess club.

After high school, he entered the army.

His sister, who married shortly after high school, was killed in a car accident in California. After her death, his mother bought a house nearby that overlooked the cemetery.

He told me all of this as one who, through all of his life, had stored up mementos and images that meant nothing to anyone but himself, but now he wanted to deposit them with someone else who might likewise encapsulate them like toxic waste in a sealed container. Having no one else to turn to, he left them with his pastor. I think though that at the time, I failed to grasp how much shame he felt about those events of his life and how difficult it had been for him to reach across the great divide in the hope that someone might care.

***

General Description

Avoidant Personality Disorder

Individuals with avoidant personality disorder are people who are adept at hiding in plain sight. They may be counted as a member on the role of a congregation, but they have a way of disappearing. Like natives in the jungle, they will watch and observe intruders into their territory without ever being seen.

The situation most likely to trigger the characteristics of an avoidant personality is any in which there are demands for close interpersonal relationships or for the utilization of extroversion skills in social settings. They long for close interpersonal relations but feel personally inadequate. They seem timid and hypersensitive to criticisms and negative evaluations. They are apt to see others as generally uncaring, and they see themselves as different or incompetent. "If others really knew me," they think, "I would be severely judged as unappealing, inept, and inferior." To avoid negative judgments, they resort to avoidance and isolate themselves from potential situations of devaluation. Social settings or places where there are likely to be arguments and conflict are their worst nightmares.

Because of their fear of embarrassment, they are often reluctant to take risks or engage in new activities. Unless they can be certain they will be liked, they resist getting involved. Because of their inhibitions, intimate relationships are often difficult for them. Though often quite intelligent, they tend to be underachievers.
Since they have a low tolerance for uncomfortable feelings, they will attempt to distract themselves or use rationalizations to

lesson feelings of loneliness or sadness.

Others are likely to view them as quiet or timid or overly sensitive. They are frequently liked but tend to elicit feelings of sympathy from others. They are often seen as someone who needs support and encouragement rather than as someone who could be approached on an equal basis as a friend.

The spiritual issue for avoidants is an essential lack of self-worth, which limits their involvement in community. They often have a history of frequent church changes and will quickly leave when they are hurt or offended in some way. They may accept the fact that in God's sight they may be "worth more than many sparrows" (Mt. 10:31), but in their own sight, they are not so sure.

Avoidant Personality Style

Those with avoidant personality style tend to be homebodies but maintain close allegiance with family and close friends. They like habit and predictable routines. They often devote themselves to hobbies that require a lot of attention and detail. They tend to be more self-conscious than most and may be overly sensitive to what others think and feel. When they do interact with others, they prefer one-on-one encounters and have often planned out in advance how they would like that interaction to proceed.

Drama Pattern for Avoidant PD

Victim becoming a rescuer becoming again a victim.

Initial role for the avoidant person is like that of someone who has been injured but tries to cover it up ("I'm doing okay."). When they perceive others might be disappointed or displeased with them, they switch to a role that seeks to be pleasing and helpful ("I'll do anything not to make you unhappy."). When rebuffed, they retreat again into the role of a victim ("I just can't deal with this. Leave me alone.").

15 DEPENDENT PERSONALITY
(CLUSTER C—ANXIOUS PARISHIONERS, CHALLENGES TO MEANINGFUL CARE)

Snapshots

Sometimes life is a result of indecision.

Melancholy settled in. Life seemed hopeless as he thought about it. There were fifteen bridges in the twelve miles between the two parishes he served. He imagined driving into the abutment, so that it would look like an accident, a result perhaps of falling asleep. But each bridge presented different opportunities or difficulties. Perhaps the next would be a better choice. Eventually, however, he found he was at his destination without having reached a decision—another failure.

The result of not making up his mind was another day in which to live, feeling helpless.

***

Martha was known as the best friend to every pastor the congregation had ever had. She was the one who could be counted upon to do whatever was needed: gather clothing for the garage sale, provide refreshments for Vacation Bible School, help the church secretary assemble the newsletter for mailing, buy supplies for the church kitchen, wash and iron the acolyte robes.

In a congregation persistently short of volunteers, she was like water in the desert. She served on a number of church committees. She seldom had anything to contribute when these committees met, but she reported regularly to the pastor the things that were said and done, and if the pastor was upset or excited by any of this information, she seemed to be in perfect harmony with these opinions.

But there was something uncomfortable about this devoted behavior. The current pastor began to wonder if she had a "real"

117

life. She began to ask her about her family. Her answers were evasive. She asked her about hobbies. She said that church work was her hobby. There wasn't anything else she enjoyed quite as much.

"Please don't volunteer for any more committees," the pastor told her.

She began to tear up. "I'm sorry," she said.

"Don't be sorry. You haven't done anything wrong," the pastor said. "I'm just concerned that you're spending too much time here."

"Okay. I'll try to do better!"

The pastor was speechless. She didn't know how to respond to that kind of obsequious behavior. She liked Martha and depended on her in many ways but was beginning to suspect that she wasn't really being helpful to her.

***

Her Facebook posting read: "Pastor's sermon today was awesome!"

Ordinarily, he would have taken that as a nice compliment and would have been glad that someone via means of social media was encouraging church attendance.

The only problem was that was not her only post about him. He seemed to show up there frequently, with comments about what she had learned in one of his Bible classes, about his sermon topics, about how he had been helpful to her in deepening her spirituality.

And that was not to mention her frequent texts to him. It was nice to be needed, but was it really his job to help her decide what color she should paint her kitchen?

It had all started when her live-in boyfriend of three years had suddenly left. Because she was understandably devastated and possibly even suicidal, he didn't mind the phone calls that sometimes came late at night. It did seem as if by patient listening, he was able to help her calm down.

He helped her focus on what she needed to do next. Since she couldn't afford the rent on her income alone, he gave her suggestions about finding an apartment that was clean and safe but more appropriate to her means. And he encouraged her to become more involved in church, which she did.

But it didn't seem to stop with that. The texts came more frequently, asking him questions about the Bible and seeking his advice about mundane things. There didn't seem to be anything romantic or flirtatious about this frequent content—he was, after all, twice her age, and he was careful about when and where he met with her. Rather, the issue became the amount of time she was requiring. He wanted to be able to pull back but sensed that in doing so she might feel abandoned.

***

He was telling me about a dream he had: he was working in a garage, with a wood chisel, carving out the trunk of a large birch tree, shaping it into a canoe.

"So what did the dream mean to you?" I asked.

"I don't know. I was wondering since I now have this call to a congregation in Minnesota, and, you know, there are a lot of lakes in Minnesota, and Indians sometimes traveled on those lakes in birch canoes—" He didn't finish the thought.

He was a pastor who had been forced to resign his previous parish after they became frustrated with his passivity and lack of any vision for the future of the congregation.

"So, you think this was like God's way of saying 'Go!'?"

"I don't know. What do you think?"

"Could be. But I'm wondering why you were working on it inside your garage rather than on the shore of the lake."

119

"That's true. That's interesting."

"And I'm wondering why you are still working on it. Sounds like it isn't finished yet, and maybe it's not ready for the lakes."

"Oh, yeah! That's so amazing. Wait a minute. Let me get my pen and write that down."

I watched, puzzled. It didn't seem that amazing to me. It was just mere speculation—an attempt to get him to delve deeper into his feelings about wanting or not wanting to go. It certainly didn't seem like something you would need to write down.

***

General Description

Dependent Personality Disorder

Individuals with dependent personality disorder exhibit a pervasive and excessive need to be taken care of by others. They are likeable, friendly, and obliging. However, they also believe that the source of all good lies outside themselves, and they hope that by remaining close to those whom they perceive as competent and by following their instructions, they will be safe. They are submissive and have an overwhelming fear of separation. They will frequently volunteer to undertake unpleasant tasks in order to gain the support and approval of others.

The situations most likely to trigger the characteristic responses of a dependent personality are any in which they are expected to demonstrate self-reliance or being alone.

They have difficulty making even simple decisions. They see themselves as weak and ineffectual and lack confidence in their own judgments and are easily suggestible. Therefore, they seek constant reassurance from those they rely upon, wanting them to take responsibility for making decisions for them.

Because they need the support of others, they have difficulty expressing any disagreement for fear they will lose support or approval. They avoid conflict or social situations in which there is likely to be tension. They tend to say "I'm sorry" a lot. They lack confidence in their own judgment.

When by themselves, they feel helpless and on edge. They have exaggerated and unrealistic fears of being unable to take care of themselves by themselves. Thus, if one relationship ends, they will urgently seek out another relationship to avoid being alone.

They often appear at first as good natured and affable, yet their tendency to gloss over the shortcomings of others is often perplexing. They may put themselves down while making excuses for the mistreatment that is heaped upon them by others. Thus, others, while sometimes at first sympathetic to them because of their desperate need for caretaking, often can become frustrated because of their inability to see their own capabilities and strengths. Instead of taking control of their own life, they resort to passive-aggressive behavior as a way to express their hurt while attempting to avoid abandonment.

Congregations are frequently attractive places for dependent personalities, as they understand fully the idea of trusting God and relying solely on a Supreme Being—though they wish God sometimes were more direct in giving advice for their everyday life. Those in ministry may at first find these to be delightful individuals, as they are often the people that can be counted upon to do the tasks, in a volunteer-starved environment, that no one else is willing to do. For those who take delight in helping others, these are the ideal recipients of this caring impulse. However, the more one takes advantage of their eager readiness to serve, the less likely one is being truly helpful to them.

Dependent Personality Style

Individuals with this personality style carefully promote harmony by being polite, agreeable, and tactful. Before making any decisions, however small, they will seek the advice of others, but eventually, they are capable of making their own decisions. They respect authority and prefer to be team members rather than leaders. They work hard to maintain relationships and are often willing to make sacrifices in order to please others who are important to them. They don't like criticism, but when it is received, they will take it to heart and attempt to apply it to themselves.

Drama Pattern for Dependent Personality Disorder

Victim switching to persecutor switching back to victim.

Dependent persons enter the drama as one who is in need of help ("I can't make up my mind. Tell me what to do."). When others attempt to push them away or ignore them, they can become demanding ("But it is your responsibility to take care of me!). And when that fails, they attempt to stay connected by pleading for sympathy ("I'm lost without you. Please help me. Why are you being so critical?").

16 OBSESSIVE-COMPULSIVE PERSONALITY (CLUSTER C—ANXIOUS PARISHIONERS, CHALLENGES TO MEANINGFUL CARE)

Snapshots

[Wife speaking about her husband to her pastor:]

"Some, I suppose, might just call them personal quirks. For a long time, that's the way I thought of them as well. That's just the way he was. If I questioned them or said anything about them, he would just get mad. Over time, I guess I just came to believe that there must be something wrong with me even to question them. But then I saw this show on TV about OCPD, and it was amazing. It was just like they knew him and were describing him.

"For one thing, he has this peculiar way of dishing up a bowl of ice cream. I think most people, when they get a scoop of ice cream, don't mind leaving little moon-like craters when they scoop out some ice cream. Not him. When he was finished dishing himself a bowl, the surface was always just as smooth as when the container was first opened. I'd be okay with that if he didn't insist that everyone else should do it the same way.

"He also always wears the same three blue shirts. I tried a couple of times getting him something different for Christmas or his birthday, but he never wore them. He complained that I had spent too much money on them. They just remained in his drawer. I don't think he ever even took the pins out. Half the time his blue shirts needed washing, but he never let me wash them for him. He insisted that he was the only one who knew just the right time to take them out of the dryer.

"Vacations are something I always dread. He complains about how much money everything costs, and he always wants to do everything the cheapest way possible. Inevitably, he gets mad about something or other, and he spends the whole vacation in a foul mood, making everyone else feel miserable as well.

"I know these are little things, and I shouldn't complain. He is a good man in many respects. He is good at his job. When people come in wanting help with their taxes, they often ask for him, even though his office is in the back. But I don't think he has any friends—not any friends in the real sense.

"For all these years, it has been like living with a powder keg of dynamite, not knowing what will light the fuse. When the kids were little, I sometimes felt that I needed to tie them to their chairs and duct tape their mouths so he wouldn't go off about something or other that they might have done.

"What I am saying is that I don't think I can put up with it anymore. I don't believe in divorce, and I have really tried. I really have. But I don't think I can take any more. I know I promised to stay with him in 'sickness and in health,' and I believe now he is truly sick, but I don't think he will admit that he is, and I don't know how to help him. Would it be wrong if I left him?"

***

"We need," said Stan, a member of the church council, "to develop a brief for incompetence." Stan's use of the word "brief" was not surprising to any member of the church council, because Stan was a corporate lawyer specializing in contracts and real estate transactions. He was known for his thoroughness in preparation for court hearings, and because he drove a Mercedes and lived in a mansion on the south side of town, members of the church were pleased that he was willing to volunteer his time to serve on the church council.

What was surprising, to Pastor Cliff at least, was the concern about "incompetence." Who did he have in mind? Why was there a need to address the subject of incompetence? Well, actually, Pastor Cliff knew exactly who the object of the brief was intended to be. Though he spoke in general terms about the need for such a document "in the case such a situation should ever arise," Pastor Glenn knew this discussion was directed at him.

Shortly after his arrival at this congregation, fresh out of seminary, he made what proved to be a pivotal mistake. He moved the clergy chair, an ornate high-back chair, out of the sanctuary and replaced it with a plain wooden chair. He thought that would be a simple symbol of the type of pastor he desired to be in their midst: approachable, available, not haughty or aloof. He didn't bother to discuss this with anyone or explain what he was doing. It seemed to him a minor thing, something most would probably not even notice.

He was wrong. The following week Stan came into his office and asked what he thought he was doing. "Do you think you own this church—that you can dispose of things or move them around without even asking permission?" After lamely trying to defend himself, Pastor Cliff apologized and returned the pastor's chair to the sanctuary the following week. But it did no good. It was clear that he did not and would not measure up to any of the standards Stan had for pastors. He was told his sermons seemed to wander without a point. He failed to dress appropriately as a pastor. He wasted his time at the town's coffee shop and failed to call on his members. He was lazy. He had no vision for the future.

Still, after the discussion about preparing a "brief of incompetence" was concluded, the matter seemed to be dropped and the storm quieted. In fact, about a month later, Pastor Cliff was invited to Stan's home for a wine and cheese party. He hoped this was an indication that the hatchet had at last been buried.

A fairly large number of people were there—not surprising, Pastor Cliff thought, given that Stan, on several occasions, was known to have thrown rather lavish parties for some of his clients. Pastor Cliff felt a little out of place in such environments but was pleased to have been included.

He soon discovered, however, that the "wine and cheese party" was in fact designed as a trial. The hearing on the matter of incompetence had commenced. Witnesses were called and led in their testimony by Stan. Notes were taken. Evidence was being gathered. Pastor Cliff sat patiently for a while, trying to keep his emotions under control, but eventually it was too much. He got up and walked out.

***

[A pastor reflecting on his ministry:]

I do not recall, now, the specific criticism a church member leveled against me, but I felt that at the root of it was an unfair expectation, and I was smarting from it. As I drove home, I defended myself: How can I do more than I am already doing?

This was not a propitious time for my wife to point out a task I had failed to do at home, but she did. I exploded. I catalogued the demands I was trying to meet and the people I was trying to please, including her and our boys. I moaned about how impossible my responsibilities were, then I marched off to another room. "Phooey on everyone," I thought. "If they don't like me the way I am, tough."

I wish I could say that such an episode has happened only once, but in my first two pastorates, it happened every year or two. The intensity of my explosions varied, but the common ingredient was unrealistic expectations. And there have been many. At times I have expected myself to excel at every facet of ministry: to read whatever book people handed to me; to make my church as fruitful as other churches; to be available at every moment; to have a perfect church.

One classic video game that gives me fits is Missile Command. On the bottom of the screen, there are six cities and three defensive missile launching sites. From the top of the screen, waves of missiles rain down to destroy them. The object of the game is defense and survival: destroy the falling explosives before they destroy you. I quickly learned to handle the first level without any challenge. The bombs fall slowly and are few in number. I can handle this, I think. Then a jarring alarm sounds. More bombs fall—faster. I can beat the second level with a sense of control, but by the end, I know I have been tested.

With the increasing difficulty of the third and fourth levels, I begin to lose control. There are more bombs. The alarm sounds at each new level. Finally, the onslaught is impossible to withstand. My cities have become craters. The game is over.

The game reminds me of my life as a pastor.

***

"Either you are going to do it my way, or I'm going to resign and leave this church!" The pastor thought that taking him up on this threat might be the ultimate solution. This individual had a habit of making that demand whenever anyone disagreed with him. He dominated nearly every committee he attended. He was a member of the church council and insisted *Robert's Rules of Order* be followed to the letter. He was also the congregation's treasurer, one of the main reasons no one wanted to challenge him on his threat. The previous treasurer had been miserable at his job and had kept a poor set of books. When he resigned, this individual stepped forward and straightened the mess. Everyone knew that if he left, there was no one else in the congregation willing or able to do his job.

He was especially irritating to staff members. If they did not do something in the way he felt it needed to be done, he brought the matter to the church council, and if it appeared that the council was unwilling to do something about the situation, he again made his resignation threat.

The pastor suspected that he operated the same way in their daily life. Everything had its proper place, and there were no exceptions.

After another occasion when the treasurer had made his threat, the pastor spoke to members of the church council concerning the power and control this person was exercising. No one, however, wanted to rock the boat. Thereafter, the pastor gave up, avoided him as much as possible, and let him have his way.

***

When Mary Katherine's husband died, a considerable amount of memorial money was contributed. Since her husband had sung in the church choir, she felt that a gift to benefit the music ministry of the congregation would be appropriate. With guidance from the pastor who was serving the congregation at that time, the money was used to purchase a set of chimes for the organ.

Over a period of time, the chimes ceased to work, and the organ console was moved so that now the organist sat with her back to the chimes. On several occasions, when she was not careful getting on or off the organ bench or when her playing became excessively exuberant, she accidently brushed into the chimes and set off a discordant clanging. Someone arrived at a solution: the chimes were tied together with panty hose.

Since the chimes had not worked for a considerable time, the current pastor suggested to the music committee that they be removed. The pastor sensed a certain reluctance on the part of the committee, but, still being rather new and since no one voiced any credible objection, he persisted and eventually prevailed.

Not long after the chimes were removed, Mary Katherine presented herself in the church office. She took a journal out of her purse and began reading: the date the chimes were installed, the feelings she had the first time they were played, the memories of her husband that came back to her.

The pastor endeavored to sympathize. Mary Katherine would have none of it. "This is about how this congregation deals with memorial money. A congregation must keep its agreements."

"But the chimes no longer work."

"That doesn't matter," Mary Katherine insisted. "The chimes were a memorial to my husband. Whether or not they were being played or not, their very presence was still a reminder of him. The congregation accepted this money under those terms, and the congregation must keep its agreements."

The pastor attempted to argue the point that they had served that purpose many years but that the needs and practices of a congregation eventually change. Mary Katherine was not at all convinced.

Soon there was a minor uproar in the congregation. Most were not unhappy to see the chimes go, but they also didn't feel it right to upset Mary Katherine. The chimes were eventually reinstalled—and a brand new pair of panty hose was used to hold them in place.

***

Super Bowl Sunday was approaching. It was suggested that perhaps a good way to reach out to the neighborhood would be to host a large Super Bowl party on the church parking lot. With a large enough TV, many could watch, refreshments could be served, and there would be an opportunity for intermingling and meeting new people. Of course, a large TV meant that one had to be rented. And that, sadly, meant going to the church treasurer. There wasn't enough time for it to go through a vote of the church council, but it was assumed the congregational treasurer would surely approve something like this. The pastor advised against it. He suggested, "Couldn't we just talk to a few people and see if we could raise enough donations for this on our own?"

He made the suggestion in hopes of avoiding a conflict. He was pretty certain the treasurer would not agree to spend the money. Before becoming congregational treasurer, he had been superintendent of the Sunday school. In that role, he had charge of the Sunday school offerings. Curiously, that amount, normally a very small amount of a congregation's operating expense, had grown to a rather significant sum and was once (and only) used, with great fanfare, for the purchase of new drapes for the educational building. Based on his apparent success and his careful shepherding and maximizing of funds, he was elected to the position of congregational treasurer. The pastor had learned, however, that he viewed the congregational treasury not as the congregation's resource, but as his responsibility: a responsibility that consisted primarily in saying "no" to any funds that could not easily be assigned to a category, that entailed some risk, or that reduced his level of control.

As the pastor feared, when the individuals requested funds from the treasurer, he refused, saying it wasn't budgeted. He also opposed approaching people individually to ask for contributions, as he believed all funds should flow through the church treasury in order to be appropriately accounted.

The parking lot party was not held.

Obsessive Compulsive Personality Disorder General Description

Most people, if at church see the three microphones in a row for the praise team singers, one of which is tilted at a slightly different angle than the other two, will likely not pay much attention to it. An individual with OCPD, however, especially if he or she is part of the music program at church, will not only notice but can hardly contain the urge to immediately go up and get them all properly aligned.

Individuals with OCPD are characterized by a pervasive preoccupation with orderliness and perfectionism. They can easily become so preoccupied with details and rules and lists and organization that the major point of an activity gets lost. Because of the need to be perfect, many of the projects they start never get completed.

The triggering event most likely to reveal the characteristics of an obsessive-compulsive personality disorder is likely to be an unstructured situation or one which demands an intimate or closer relationship.

Obsessive-compulsives are often particularly good with numbers, as numbers are reliable and predictable. They are much less successful when it comes to working with people. Because they exercise a good deal of self-discipline, often to an extreme, they are often suspicious and distrustful of others who appear to lack the sufficient strictness they themselves find as necessary for control. They are reluctant to delegate, unless others are willing to do things exactly their way. When others don't do what they want, they become easily frustrated and demanding.

They see rules as absolute and necessary. Thus, they can be overly conscientious, scrupulous, and inflexible about morality, ethics, and values. When they see traditions broken, they become extremely uncomfortable and may vilify and scold those they see as upsetting the right way to do things. On the other hand, they tend to hold authority figures in high regard and are deferential to them.

They often have difficulty discarding worn-out or worthless

objects. This sometimes leads to wearing the same articles of clothing over and over again. Some have been known to wear the same underwear for several days in a row.

Typically, others view them as stubborn and rigid. They have few friends. Some become annoyed at their inability to see the bigger picture. Others become frustrated with their demanding and controlling behavior. Efforts to please them seldom succeed.

Obsessive-compulsives are sometimes viewed as loyal church members because of their strong beliefs about ethics and morals. On the other hand, when placed in positions of authority, they often become controlling and demanding and incapable of being flexible. Spiritually, they tend to view God as stingy, providing only limited resources and requiring strict obedience.

Obsessive-Compulsive Personality Style

Individuals with obsessive-personality style take pride in doing all tasks well, giving attention to every detail. They tend to want things done "just right" and in a precise manner but have developed some tolerance for others who have different ideas. They are dedicated individuals who work hard and take pride in their work. They are no-nonsense individuals who seldom need much encouragement from others. Having strong beliefs, they have a sincere desire to do everything in the right way. Thrifty and careful about spending, they tend to save and collect objects, but though they spend little on themselves, but are sometimes willing to share generously with others.

Drama Pattern for the Obsessive-Compulsive PD

Rescuer to persecutor.

Initial role is often that of a rescuer ("Let me handle it. I know what to do."). When criticized or suggestions made on how things might be done differently, the switch is made to persecutor ("But that is not right. There is only one way to do this, and I know the right way.").

17 CARE AND MANAGEMENT FOR INDIVIDUALS WITH PERSONALITY DISORDERS

In ancient times, a few individuals have learned to overcome their fear of snakes, studying their characteristics and becoming skillful in handling and caring for them without fear of personal harm. Since many have a natural fear of snakes, this often led those individuals with knowledge of snakes to be viewed as having magical or supernatural powers. Such perhaps were the Egyptian magicians who, copying Aaron, were able to turn their staffs into snakes (Ex. 7:11). Possibly, they had learned the trick of pinching a certain nerve in the snake's neck, which temporarily paralyzed it. The book of Psalms likewise makes mention of "snake charmers" (Ps. 58:5).

Snake charmers are still a popular tourist attraction in India and some parts of the Middle East and appear to make a poisonous shake rise out of a basket and dance by playing a reed-like instrument. In reality, the snake doesn't dance, as it has no ears. It is responding to the vibrations but is unable to attack because the charmer knows the exact distance that places him just beyond the reach of its strike. It is an example of what they learned about snakes through their many years of study and observation. Originally, as part of their training, snake charmers learned to treat snake bites, and, since they also learned proper snake handling techniques, they were often called upon to remove serpents from homes.

Rather than learning how to "charm" difficult parishioners, the typical manner of dealing with personality disorders in congregations has been a form of exorcism—get rid of the one who personifies evil, who acts in ways that seem beyond the bounds of normal human behavior. Difficult members are sometimes told they are *persona non grata* and are barred from the premises. Likewise, pastors who are judged to be incapable of meeting expectations are "fired," told to leave. Little or no effort is made to negotiate differences or to resolve problems. Possibly there are times when these actions become necessary. But is a form of exorcism always the best option?

Working with and providing care for individuals with features of personality disorders in congregational settings begins with recognizing general characteristics.

General Guidelines for Recognizing Personality Disorders

Reacting to an individual with a personality disorder in the way one typically responds is at best unhelpful and quite likely the beginning of a chaotic relationship. You will soon find yourself thinking, feeling, and acting in ways that are atypical for you. They, on the other hand, will continue to think, feel, and act in the ways they always do. They will be true to type. Therefore, the first step in being able to manage these relationships into a more helpful direction is to be able to recognize the presence of a personality disorder.

Some detail has already been provided about ten different types of personality disorder, but it is useful first of all to think more globally and less specifically. How do you know whether or not a particular individual may have some type of personality disorder? Again, the purpose is not to label or to officially diagnose but to raise your awareness so that you can recognize when you may be called upon to exercise relationship skills that you would not normally need to utilize in interacting with the majority of people. Several general characteristics are applicable to most personality disorders. Knowing these can alert you to the need to pay closer attention when certain situations arise.

1) *Individuals with personality disorders have difficulty assuming an appropriate level of responsibility.* Either they have difficulty acknowledging or accepting their role in problems that have occurred and resort instead to justifications and rationalizations to defend their actions, or they resort to excessive self-blame, assuming responsibility for actions and events that were really the fault of others. Most of us, when criticized, will often initially respond in a similar fashion, but individuals with personality disorders have difficulty rising above these instinctive reactions. Their need to defend their way of being negates any attempt to find solutions.

Fixing blame, either to others or to themselves, becomes more important than gaining understanding about self and others and learning from experience.

2) Individuals with personality disorders typically lack empathy. Driven primarily by their own needs, they have difficulty recognizing or understanding the needs of others. Some, like antisocial or narcissistic, are adept at sensing the needs of others, but they use this knowledge primarily for the purpose of exploitation. They have little capacity for empathy. When they do occasionally sense that someone else may be hurt, frustrated, or angry with them, they either show too little remorse or they overreact, making grandiose apologies in an effort to further manipulate.

3) Individuals with personality disorders lack problem-solving skills. They are stuck in a certain way of behaving and continue to repeat those behaviors no matter how often they find themselves in the same situation over and over again. The repetition seems to confirm their beliefs that the assumptions they have made about themselves or others is correct.

4) They see themselves as acting out of necessity. They are reacting to the way they perceive the world to be. That their view of the world might be wrong or incomplete never enters their frame of reference.

5) They generate conflict and frustration in most of their relationships, not just in their relationship with you. If this is a personality-driven trait, not a situational one, observe how often the pattern is repeated.

6) For these individuals, an entire dysfunctional system seems to activate whenever they encounter something in their world view that appears wrong. The system often includes unusual thoughts, feelings, behaviors, and fantasies. The ten types of personality disorders in effect describe the different content of ten different reactive systems to a threat of some kind. A person with a personality disorder will always activate the same dysfunctional system and will not think and act one way with one individual or situation and another way with another individual or situation.

General Guidelines for Working with Personality-Disordered Individuals

In most cases, you will experience some kind of emotional response when encountering someone with a personality disorder. You may feel puzzled, frustrated, angry, hurt, surprised, or some combination of all of the above. Pay attention. These feelings are not guides to behavior. In fact, if you act on them, more often than not you will quickly worsen the situation. Rather, take them as alert signals. Go home and think about them. Is someone you have just encountered reacting to a particular situation, or are they acting out of their own nature, their way of being? Is the issue not the issue, and does it go to something deeper? Does it really relate more to them than to anything you did or said? If so, it may well be you are in a relationship with one of the ten types of individuals that we have been describing.

So, what do you do if you have identified someone in your congregation who likely has a personality disorder? Recommending therapy is one option. Therapy can provide help for individuals with personality disorders. Several treatment modalities for working with these disorders have been developed and have proven to be quite successful. However, because individuals with personality disorders seldom think they have a problem, it is often difficult to get them into therapy, and once in therapy, they often have many excuses to drop out. Personality change comes slowly, and to be effective these treatments require regular therapy sessions: often twice a week for a period of nine months to a year. Furthermore, this kind of treatment may not be covered by mental health insurance and therefore may be costly. In severe cases, some form of intervention may be necessary to get them into treatment, eliciting the help of others in their life who also recognize the problems. As part of the preparation for an intervention, it would be important to locate a therapist who specializes in treatment of personality disorders and be prepared to meet objections related to cost and time commitment.

If, however, therapy is not an option, should clergy on their own attempt to treat or change a person who is suspected of having a personality disorder? This is usually not a good option; time commitment and lack of training are among the reasons it would not be advisable to attempt this.

Thus, the preferred approach may be to practice management and informed pastoral care. Here the goal is not to figure out how to change this individual. Rather, the task is to figure out what adaptations you need to make within yourself in order to be more effective in working with him or her. Chances are, your typical way of relating to others will not produce the kind of results that you expect. On the other hand, changing your own behavior patterns can serve to stop repetitive cycles, establish appropriate boundaries, limit potential damage, and, in some cases, result in caring for another in a way that is truly helpful.

First and foremost, management involves not being drawn into the drama cycle. The dynamics and emotional experience are totally different for one who is in the audience watching the drama and one who is in the play actively participating. While in the audience, you may experience the emotion being acted out on stage, but you understand you are not part of that drama. Likewise, by staying out of the drama cycle typically created by these individuals, the drama may continue even without you, but the emotional effect upon yourself is much less, and the more severe negative effects of the drama both for the individual and the congregation may be ameliorated.

Many are drawn to the calling of ministry because they care about people and empathize with them. But empathy can be a trap and is not always the best way to be helpful to individuals with personality disorders. Consider several examples:

A dependent frequently approaches you, seeking advice. Her son is repeatedly getting into trouble at school. She doesn't know whether she needs to be stricter with him or provide more love and attention. This becomes an ongoing saga. She also asks questions about what you said in your sermon, trying to find ways to apply that to her life. You listen carefully and offer suggestions. She takes your advice seriously and tells you often how much you are helping her. This is all mildly flattering. You went into ministry hoping to care for people and to make a difference in their lives, and here is a concrete example of it actually taking place. But if you fail to recognize the dependent drama pattern and operate on empathy alone, you won't recognize that you are being set up for the inevitable drama switch. By making her increasingly dependent on you, sooner or later you will fail her: if not while you are still serving in that congregation, when you eventually leave. She will then experience an even deeper sense of abandonment, and her dependency needs will increase. Working with dependents requires mixing helpfulness with a degree of distancing. Be attentive but avoid making their decisions for them and occasionally make yourself unavailable. In so doing you will be expressing your confidence in their own abilities to make decisions and to work problems out for themselves.

A borderline wants to become your best friend. Ministry can be a lonely place, and this appears to be someone you can laugh with, go with to sports events, and converse with about subjects that have nothing at all to do with congregational issues. You are glad to have such a friend, and this seems reciprocated, as frequently you receive gifts and other tokens of appreciation from him. Once you receive a message on your phone that he has called, but because it is rather late, you decide to wait until the next day before returning the call. When you do call, you are taken aback by the storm of anger that confronts you. Empathy might lead you to attempt to be understanding of this person's feelings and to apologize, but empathy with borderlines is the first step onto the roller coaster of emotions that will lead you to alternate wildly between trying desperately to be caring and understanding while feeling angry and frustrated. When you understand that you are interacting with a borderline, know that he wants to put you into the role of both best friend and worst enemy. Avoid that drama switch. Your best course is to be consistent, with clear expectations and boundaries. Be this individual's pastor, who is neither overly friendly nor overly provoked and frustrated with him.

A narcissistic pastor has recruited you to be the director of youth at his large church. It is an exciting opportunity, made even more so by the pastor's dramatic description of the past accomplishments of the congregation and his vision for the future. Excitement at the opportunity, however, soon is converted into stress to meet the high expectations. The senior pastor berates you for spending too much time listening to and working with the needs of individual teens and not enough time planning and promoting mission trips, which he is eager to publicize. This flips the drama switch and leads to you eventually lose all respect for him because of his tendency to run over people. In this case, a normal tendency to empathy leads to anger and rage at the way he treats people. However, recognizing you are dealing with a narcissist could lead to charting a path where occasional expressions of admirations, even if partially feigned, enable you to work with him and operate your ministry at a respectful distance, neither dependent on his approval nor overly wounded by his occasional need to put you down in some way.

A histrionic parishioner dresses seductively and occasionally flirts with you. You might be led either to reciprocate and offer compliments, because they are clearly seeking recognition, or to avoid this person altogether, recognizing danger. However, recognizing that you are dealing with a histrionic leads you to be careful of any recognition or reward of the individual's attention-seeking behavior while also refraining from embarrassing or shaming that person, which is the drama switch he or she expects.

A paranoid parishioner accuses you of being like "a bull in a china shop" because you added a children's message to the worship service, which he regards as pure entertainment and not properly worshipful, and because you used a portion of the church property to build a labyrinth as a place for people to meditate, which he declared was unbiblical and decidedly "New Agey." Since you might find the attempt to be empathetic with this point of view difficult, particularly since he presented it in such an accusatory and annoying manner, you might easily become hurt and find yourself distancing yourself from him. But that would simply trip the drama switch he expects. Recognizing that you are working with a paranoid calls for a different strategy. Laugh with him about his accusations. Give him a Chicago Bears hat while wearing a Chicago Bulls hat, indicating that is their differing perspective about the future of the congregation. Let him know that you are thankful for people who guard the traditions of the church, because you recognize these as important and want to find ways to respect them. In other words, he expects you to become his enemy. Treat him as a friend.

Some additional guidelines in working with personality disorders:

Remember that the issue is usually not the issue. When narcissists attempt to shame you, realize that being defensive is not likely to help. Rather, observe how they are attempting to use an issue (whatever it is) in an attempt to justify their self-image. When avoidants attempt to get you to act on their behalf, point out how their avoidance of an issue only perpetuates the problem. When obsessive-compulsives complain that you are not doing things the right way, rather than defending your actions or arguing with them, wonder aloud with them about what happens when things are not done in the right way.

Whenever possible, outline for them cause and effect: "Have you ever noticed that no matter how hard you strive to make everything perfect, they never seem to turn out that way?" (obsessive-compulsive). "Did you see the way people start looking around and stop making conversations with you whenever you start talking about your favorite hobby of collecting pills?" (schizotypal). "Have you ever wondered why the other women of the congregation look at you the way they do when you dress that way?" (histrionic). People with personality disorders frequently are unable to make these cause-and-effect connections. Making such connections clear to them can be helpful.

When attacked, don't respond in kind or attempt to defend yourself. As soon as you do so, you have entered into the expected drama role. Instead, try to keep the focus on solving the problem. "So you think I should have made follow-up visits on your aunt Maude after she got out of the hospital. You're probably right. But let's talk about how we can prevent something like that happening in the future. Is there a better way to get the word out when someone may need a pastoral visit, so that it isn't simply a matter of guesswork? Could we perhaps find volunteers who would telephone people after they were discharged and pass those names on to me when they believed a pastoral visit was important?" Individuals with personality disorders find problem solving difficult, and it won't happen unless you take the initiative.

Maintain your emotional arousal level lower than theirs. They say angrily as they are leaving church: "I thought it was very distasteful of you to tell a joke in a sermon."

You say, "Okay."

They say, "I hope you don't ever do it again."

You say, "I'll think on it."

They say, "If you ever do it again, I'll leave this church."

You say, "Okay."

Remember, what they say is really not personal. They do it all the time to all kinds of people in their life. To think or act like you are being singled out is a mistake.

Especially when working with staff members or congregational leaders, establish behavioral covenants (a sample behavioral covenant is found in Appendix B). The covenants should be clear and specific. They should cover such things as the expectations for attending meetings, being on time, the procedure for handling complaints, not responding to anonymous complaints, deadline of meeting agenda additions, direct communication, and so forth. This will often feel legalistic and pedantic, but it is essential for dealing with personality disorders, because disorders love to dance on agreements: exceptions are expected, excuses are made. But with written agreements in place, boundaries are established.

"You were late for the meeting."

"Yes, I had an important phone call to make."

"Okay, but you were late for the meeting."

"You expect us to be here even when we get sick or when someone is dying?"

"No, but you weren't sick or dying, and you were late for the meeting."

"You are being unreasonable."

"Okay. But you were late for the meeting."

Being strict and unbending in such a way doesn't come naturally to many who are in ministry. There is often a fear of being regarded as stubborn and demanding. But it is important to ask oneself: Which is more important to you: to be seen in a good light by everyone or to act in ways that is best for the whole of the congregation?

Know what you are trying to accomplish and stay focused on that goal. Personality disorders are more interested in drama than in solutions. Once you become a part of the drama, goals go out the window.

Be careful with empathy when dealing with victims. Empathy is a tool for caring for those who have endured losses. Those, however, who use their victimization as a justification for their behavior are not benefitted by empathy. Ignore but don't criticize those who attempt to use their victim status as a means to gain power and attention.

Beware those who expect special attention or demand exceptions be made for them. Often these are efforts to draw you into their drama.

Even when it is necessary to be guarded in your relationships with some individuals, continue to treat them civilly and, when appropriate, compliment them.

When it is necessary to criticize someone, do it specifically, directly, and briefly. Don't speak in generalities but describe the specific action or behavior that raised concern. Raise the issue directly with the individual and refrain from talking about it to others. Do it once and then drop the matter. Don't be surprised if he or she is angry or hurt. Understand that it may take time to absorb that you are criticizing a specific action, not them as a person.

Develop peer relationships with those with whom you can consult and from whom you can obtain objective feedback. Congregations in and of themselves can become closed worlds. When caught up in dramas involving personality disorders, it is easy to lose your bearings and begin to doubt yourself. Don't wait to look for someone with whom you can obtain advice and receive objective feedback until after problems have arisen, because by then it is often too late. This needs to be a priority when you first begin a ministry in a given place. Along with learning the names of the congregational leaders, finding where you will take your car to be worked on, who will be your doctor, and those other tasks that automatically go along with establishing oneself in a community, find a mentor or peer with whom you can meet on a regular basis.

18 TUNING IN: SPECIFIC GUIDELINES FOR SPECIFIC PERSONALITIES

If you were a herpetologist caring for a large variety of snakes, it would be important to know something about each, as their dietary needs, frequency of eating, and safety precautions will vary for each species. In a similar manner, once you have identified a pattern that indicates the likely presence of a personality disorder, it is helpful to identify which kind, as it will determine the best way to provide pastoral care and management in a congregational setting.

Here are some guidelines. When I first read through the following guidelines after I had written them, they seemed much more dogmatic and smug than I had intended. They are not intended as hard and fast rules. Human beings are complex. Even the same individual does not always respond in the same way to the same circumstance. In many cases, just knowing that you are relating to a person with a personality disorder may be enough. They are acting true to type. Don't expect them to be different than they are. However, if you wish to experiment with changing the manner in which you relate to them, these guidelines offer different strategies to try.

Cluster A Personality (Odd, Eccentric—Providing Challenges to Congregational Assimilation):

Suggestions for Pastoral Care and Management with Paranoid Personalities

To avoid being caught in the drama, resist becoming either a rescuer or a persecutor. Individuals with paranoid personality disorder will often become involved in congregational life when they believe the congregation is in some kind of danger. They are uncomfortable in seeing congregations spend money for new outreach programs or building projects. When numbers decline, they are quick to see doom and gloom. They see themselves taking on the role of rescuing the congregation from imminent danger. When that role is not embraced by others, they quickly become victims, putting others into the role of judge.

In resisting the drama, clergy and congregational leaders should remain neutral regarding the fears and accusations paranoids make. To confront and argue with their interpretation of events places one in the expected role of persecutor, and the drama plays on. Rather, take a neutral stance. If they imply, "This congregation is going to hell in a hand basket," respond with something like, "Really? Do you see it that way?" When possible, acknowledge the accuracy of their observations without validating the paranoid conclusions they draw from those observations. Treat them respectfully without patronization or being overly complimentary or encouraging.

Some congregations have assigned individuals like this to the role of their "designated worrier." This can be done playfully, acknowledging the need for someone to be on the lookout for potential dangers, while at the same time not being controlled by their fear.

If you are able to establish a respectful relationship with them, whenever possible demonstrate curiosity about their view of themselves as righteous but mistreated by others and their view of others as interfering and devious. Wonder with them about their lack of trust and what it means to them that God is trustworthy. Ask them about past experiences when they have been right about their suspicions of the unreliability and malevolent intent of others and whether they can recall any instances when they were wrong. Joke with them about whether or not it would be possible for them to be distrustful of their mistrustful thoughts.

Suggestions for Pastoral Care and Management with Schizoids

Avoid becoming a judge in their drama pattern. Be patient! They may appear boring or uninteresting at times, but they often have much to contribute if given the chance. In conversations with them, don't be put off by long periods of silence. From time to time, they will throw out clues to see if you are attentive. Be attentive to any sign of distress or hint of emotion that can indicate an opportunity to dig deeper.

Whenever the opportunity presents itself, attempt to discover what things are important to them, what they care about, and what options they have for keeping those activities and resources in their life.

When inviting them to participate in a congregational activity, don't take a "no" response as definitive. Often it requires repeated invitations before they are convinced you are sincere.

Encouragement to utilize quiet times and meditation rather than reading devotional material as ways to deepen their relationship with God may serve to enrich their spiritual life.

Sometimes providing care involves working with family members who are upset by their level of detachment.

Suggestions for Pastoral Care and Management with Schizotypals

To avoid the drama, resist becoming either a rescuer or a persecutor. Maintain a tolerant and open style in your relationships with them. Treat them as "normal" and attempt to find roles for them in congregational life where they can be accepted, despite their occasionally strange thinking. When they express ideas that seem odd or unusual, neither validate nor invalidate their thoughts. If some of their behavior needs to be corrected because they are unaware of how they are being perceived, do so carefully and politely and follow up in order to make sure the corrective action was not understood as judgment but as advice given with care.

If they hold eccentric beliefs, be cautious about challenging those beliefs, even if they are of questionable validity. Rather, try to understand what their belief means for them and why it is important.

When possible, learn more about the practical aspects of their life. Are their living conditions satisfactory? Do they need assistance with food stamps or legal aid? Getting to know their primary care provider, usually a relative, can also be helpful in finding appropriate ways to relate to them.

Cluster B Personalities (Dramatic—Creating Congregational Conflict and Turmoil):

Suggestions for Pastoral Care and Management with Antisocials

Avoid the drama by not being a victim in need of their intervention. Be straightforward with them and remain skeptical. Take nothing on faith or based solely on their word. Listen to their schemes and show an interest—it helps you get more information about them—but resist the sales pitch. When you feel as if you are being manipulated, don't just avoid the manipulation, name it to them as manipulation. Ignore their attempts to frighten you by threats and be aware of any feeling that you need to be liked by them. Remain indifferent to both their praise and their hostility. Resistance to their attempts to manipulate you may succeed at least in making you an object of curiosity to them. They are more used to either being complied with or rejected outright, not resisted with a firm gentleness.

Avoid practicing "cheap grace" with them. Forgiveness is often a meaningless concept to them as most often they don't feel they have done anything wrong. Rather, emphasize consequences. Repeatedly point out to them how their behavior has had a negative effect not only upon others but also upon them. The idea of genuine forgiveness is a concept difficult for them to grasp. They live by conning others and assume that everyone else does the same. Thus, they will be suspicious of anyone who grants them acceptance, wondering what game they are playing and what they hope to get out of it.

The challenge for faith communities is to not be deceived by the deceptive ploys of antisocials while at the same time recognizing the scared, unloved person their brashness tries to conceal. Extend the gift of grace if and when that scared and unloved part of themselves makes an appearance, but for their benefit as well as the congregation's, whenever possible, prevent them from holding any position that gives them power, particularly any position that involves finances. In certain situations, more vulnerable members of the congregation need to be actively shielded from their preying activities.

Suggestions for Pastoral Care and Management with Borderlines

To avoid the drama, resist the temptation to become either a rescuer or a persecutor of individuals with borderline personality disorder. Establishing clear boundaries is essential. Be consistent and firm about when you are available to listen to them and the degree to which you are willing to help. Provide consistency. Resist manipulation. When they are operating appropriately within the boundaries you have set, listen sympathetically and understandingly. Validate the feelings they express but not necessarily the accuracy of those feelings—i.e., acknowledge that they appear to be feeling sad, abandoned, mistreated, or misused, even if the particular situation doesn't justify feeling that way. When they become frustrated with you and try to goad you into an argument, resist. Do not be surprised if the next day the anger is completely gone and forgotten.

When borderlines are in a crisis and exhibiting suicidal or self-injury behavior, intervene as needed and seek to get them appropriate help.

Suggestions for Pastoral Care and Management with Histrionics

To avoid being caught in the drama, resist becoming a rescuer. Express appropriate interest and empathy and do not challenge them too quickly. Pay more attention to their behavior than to the content of their words.

The need for reassurance is the need that drives histrionics' provocative behavior, and thus it is important to provide them with a modicum of affirmation while also carefully maintaining boundaries. Congregations easily become places where histrionic behavior leads to sexual misconduct. Religion involves expressions of love, caring, fellowship, and personal sharing. These expressions can easily become eroticized. Clergy who haven't practiced meaningful self-care and are experiencing burnout are particularly susceptible. It is important to give careful attention to when and where individuals who are possibly histrionic are seen. Do not compliment histrionics on their appearance or on their attention-seeking behavior but find some other aspect of their character or behavior that deserves commendation.

As opportunity presents itself, wonder with them why it is necessary for them to be loved by everyone in order to be worthwhile. Often histrionics were sexually abused as a child or have had a negative sexual experience sometime in the past and have generalized that experience into "all men" or "all women." Challenge this "all or nothing" attitude by encouraging them to think of exceptions. Explore with them how they understand, "When I am weak, then I am strong" (II Cor. 12:10).

When histrionics' attention-seeking behavior creates major problems, it may become necessary to remove them from a position of influence within the congregation. In such situations, it can be assumed that there will be resistance both from the individual and his or her admirers. However, most likely you are dealing with a person whose need for attention is insatiable, and the problems associated with this will not go away.

Suggestions for Pastoral Care and Management with Narcissists

To avoid becoming part of the drama, stay out of the victim role. As Wayne Oates put it in his book *Behind the Masks*, the alternatives for existing peacefully and without confrontation with a narcissist are few: 1) ignore them; 2) stay out of contractual negotiations with them; or 3) listen without responding as they boast and compliment themselves.

Actually, to show some level of interest in their

accomplishments and abilities may be necessary to avoid hostility or rage, remembering that behind their boasting and self-aggrandizement lies a fiercely defended vulnerable self. Wounded narcissists can become dangerous. When they endeavor to impress you, show an interest in their accomplishments and abilities while remaining politely indifferent to their need to receive praise. Be friendly with them but not overly solicitous.

If troubles begin to occur, present them with specific facts and details about the consequences of their behavior while also brainstorming with them to find a better way to get what they want.

When it is impossible to help the individual directly, shift the focus to how to protect others. This may involve both providing emotional and spiritual support for those who have experienced distress resulting from their interactions with a narcissist as well as removing the individual from positions of influence and control in the congregation.

Cluster C Personalities (Anxious—Challenges to Meaningful Care)

Suggestions for Pastoral Care and Management with Avoidants

Remain apart from avoidants' drama by resisting the temptation to become judgmental. Avoidants expect to be disliked and others to become critical. Therefore, use a gentle, nonconfrontational style with them. Show an interest in them and be accepting. Some degree of self-disclosure may help them to know what you are thinking, and that you are able to identify with their struggles.

Provide them with support and encouragement and present them with realistic options. Promise them little (they will be doubly hurt by broken promises) but do more. Don't expect or demand that they do more than that with which they are comfortable. Attempt to find a role for them in congregational life that requires little interpersonal interaction but enables them to contribute in their own way, thus helping them to feel they are a part of the community.

Suggestions for Pastoral Care and Management with Dependents

Avoid becoming a part of the drama by resisting the desire to be eager to help. Question your own need to be needed. Does this person in some way, perhaps only vaguely felt, remind you of ways you have been mistreated or ignored in the past? In trying to care for them, are you really only trying to care for yourself?

Instead of trying to solve all their problems, employ a pleasant supportive style but avoid giving advice or making suggestions for them. Set realistic boundaries for them as well as for yourself. Advise them against taking on too much or giving too much of themselves. Be clear with them what you can and cannot do for them. Have a realistic expectation that progress, if any, will be slow.

As you have opportunity, explore their feelings of helplessness and inadequacy. Question the accuracy of their fears of being alone and independent. Encourage and strengthen their ability to say "no." When they are seeking advice about a particular decision, brainstorm with them the pros and cons of various alternatives but avoid drawing any final conclusions for them.

Make a point to not compliment them for anything agreeable they say or do. Rather, look for any occasion when they voice a disagreement or fail to do something that was expected of them and compliment them effusively for their ability to take a stand.

Suggestions for Pastoral Care and Management with Obsessive Compulsives

Obsessive-compulsives respect authority. Use it as necessary to challenge unproductive behaviors. Acknowledge that there are certain "right" and "proper" ways to do things and state what those are. In conversations with them, don't hesitate to interrupt when they seem to have become fixated on one issue. Change the subject frequently. Whenever possible, talk with them about the big picture and of how their role and contribution to the congregation fits into that larger perspective.

Compliment them on things they do well, but do so reservedly, being careful not to reinforce behavior that could become controlling in nature.

As the opportunity presents itself, ask them about their fears. Question them about what they think would happen if their greatest fears came into being, and then reason with them both why it is unlikely their greatest fear will happen and why, if it should, what it means to them that God would still be present. Wonder with them about the difference between always trying to do things the right way and what the Bible talks about as a "righteousness by faith apart from the deeds of the law."

Whenever possible, avoid having them serve in positions in the congregation where their anxiety and need for control increases both their anxiety and the anxiety of the congregation.

19 CONGREGATIONS AS DISORDERED PERSONALITIES

"Elmer has been retired for half a dozen years from his job as a tool and die operator at a machinist factory. He is happy about the extra time this has provided, gets together for coffee with some of his friends at the local McDonald's, and volunteers for the meals-on-wheels program. He has a friendly smile, and people like him.

"He lives modestly in the same house he has inhabited for the past thirty years. It shows the signs of its age: the coral pink fixtures in the bathroom have never been updated, and much of the furniture shows the unmistakable signs of wear, but it is clean and tidy.

"Those who don't know him well are often surprised at the depth of his knowledge and his variety of interests, much more than one would expect of someone with nothing more than a high school education who spent his life as a blue-collar worker, though it is probably wise to stay away from the subjects of politics, as he can become quite vocal in his conservative beliefs.

"There is a depth of sadness, however, behind his friendly smiles. His wife died four years ago, and though he has five children and nine grandchildren, he has limited contact with any of them. The change came gradually, but now the difference is unmistakable. The memories of a house filled with children's voices and teenagers and their friends are long gone. For the most part, it hasn't been arguments or disagreements that created the distance from his children that he is experiencing, though at times he can be quite stubborn. Rather, it is more a matter that they developed other interests and moved to other cities. They still frequently contact him for birthdays and Christmas, but the absences in between are often long and heartbreaking. He would like somehow to bridge the gap that exists, but he doesn't know how."

That is a description of the personality of the congregation that I attend to my wife. I had told her about a book I had read by Janet Cawley, titled *Who Is Our Church: Imagining Congregational Identity*, in which she suggests that congregations can be thought of as personalities. My wife was dubious, thinking it impossible to describe a congregation that consists of many different people as a single identity, so I gave her the above description, and she had to admit, "Yes, that's it!"

It may be difficult to understand or describe exactly what creates or transmits a congregational personality. Perhaps it can be contributed to "memes," the idea first proposed by Richard Dawkins, namely, that certain cultural ideas are transmitted from one to another though conversations, symbols, rituals, and gestures. Systems theory, with its concepts that relationships are the means for both regulating and transmitting anxiety no doubt also provides some explanation, but whatever the means of transmission, one can hardly doubt its existence in congregations. How else does one explain how congregations, despite the coming and going of many people, seem to maintain a certain identity that is almost immediately recognizable to first-time visitors? Or how else does one explain, as many consultants have discovered when involved in congregations in the aftermath of sexual misconduct, that the current misconduct issue is often not the first time such an event happened in the history of that congregation. Do pastors accept a call to that congregation with the intent of acting out sexually? Not likely. Or how does one explain why certain congregations who had a negative experience with a pastor some forty years ago still exhibit a mistrust of all of their pastors?

It is often helpful for pastors to think of their congregation as a single personality. It is sometimes difficult to love some of the people within the congregation. But a pastor is called to love the church. Within that congregation, pastors will experience many different kinds of people. Some they will love dearly. Some they will hardly know. And others will greatly try their patience, or, quite frankly, even dislike. But the task is to love the congregation as a whole, as an identity whom they have come to serve. We instinctively know how to do this with individuals we know well. We know how to deal with an uncle who may be always grouchy and pessimistic and with a little child who always wants to be the center of attention. We are often able to overlook many of their foibles because we know them at a deeper level. Understanding your congregation's personality can provide a similar perspective.

But, if congregations have personalities, then presumably congregations can also have personality disorders, a pervasive pattern of thinking and behavior that appears inflexible and inhibitive of problem solving.

The same ten personality disorders that apply to individuals may presumably apply to the personalities of congregations. If one were to hypothesize what the traits might be, they perhaps would look something like this:

The paranoid congregation is one in which its members:

1) frequently suspect the motives of the pastor or other congregational leaders, believing without sufficient basis that they are being exploited or deceived;
2) are unwilling to volunteer for fear that they will be criticized or taken advantage of;
3) misconstrue information and comments in a way that reads hidden or threatening messages into them;
4) persistently hold grudges and dwell on past slights or hurts; and
5) are quick to take simple statements or innocuous actions personally, to which they react instinctively with anger and aggression.

The schizoid congregation is one in which its members:

1) have few if any close relationships or friendships;
2) have little interest in getting involved with others in working on projects or holding office;
3) have difficulty describing what, if anything, their church membership means to them;
4) seem unmotivated either by congregational successes or failures; and
5) are perceived by visitors as well as others in the community as being aloof, cold, and unfriendly.

The schizotpal congregation is one in which its members

1) appear odd or unusual to the broader community in which it is located, perhaps because its entire membership consists almost entirely of the homeless, LGBT individuals, new immigrants, or other clearly binding identity that is not part of the social mainstream;
2) practice their faith with rituals and practices that appear unusual and nontraditional to others of the same religion;
3) have relationships that appear friendly but are often superficial; and
4) tend unrealistically to think of their church as special and superior to all others.

The antisocial congregation is one in which its pastor or some of its members or leaders:

1) frequently deceive others through repeated lies, misrepresentations, and abuse of power;
2) will misuse or mistreat some members for their own personal advantage or gain;
3) are often more interested in financial gain than in service; and
4) strongly resist any attempt at suitable accountability and oversight.

The borderline congregation is one in which its members:

1) impulsively start many projects but seldom finish any of them;
2) are fearful of survival and eagerly latch on to potential new members but quickly find fault with them;
3) have no clear identity as a congregation and jump from one project to another; and
4) are continually fearful of survival and quickly become angry at their pastor or leaders whenever they feel abandoned by them.

The histrionic congregation is one in which its members:

1) give undue attention to externals—repainting the church or redoing the constitution rather than dealing directly with problems;
2) will eagerly volunteer for activities that will put them in a highly visible role, but are not interested in attending traditional Bible classes or practicing spiritual disciplines;
3) experience frequent conflict, often over details that don't seem to matter; and
4) like to put on extravaganzas, elaborate Christmas pageants, catered dinners, and Easter celebrations that can be publicized in newspapers and talked about in the neighborhoods.

The narcissistic congregation is one in which its members:

1) have a grandiose sense of importance and exaggerate the accomplishments and achievements of the congregation;
2) believe that they are unique and can only be understood by pastors and congregational leaders of other congregations of similar size and importance;
3) have a sense of entitlement that expects special treatment or recognition by others, which in turn sometimes leads to justification of illegal or unethical behavior; and
4) believe that members of other congregations are envious of them.

The avoidant congregation is one in which its members:

1) are generally unwilling to get involved;
2) have few activities beyond a weekly worship;
3) are fearful of being disliked by their pastor and by others and will sometimes act in ways that will confirm this suspicion; and
4) generally have a low opinion of themselves and the significance of their congregation.

The dependent congregation is one in which its members:

1) regularly postpone making decisions of any kind;
2) are overly polite and fearful of causing hurt feelings to anyone;
3) are generally willing to volunteer and serve as long as someone else makes the decisions for them; and
4) are often ruled by a few strong minded individuals whom they allow to take charge even though they often don't agree with them or even like them.

The obsessive-compulsive congregation is one in which its members:

1) are preoccupied with rules and orderliness to the extent that the purpose of activities is often lost;
2) exhibit a degree of perfectionism and are overly critical when others do not measure up to that standard;
3) are overly conscientious and inflexible about matters or morals and ethics and emphasize the law over grace;
4) tend not to discard old church furniture and decorations even when no longer used;
5) have a few individuals who do most of the work because of their unwillingness to delegate to others who might not do it as well or the same way as them;
6) are typically rigid and stubborn; and
7) are overly cautious about spending and financial matters, preferring to have money in the bank rather than spend it on outreach or mission projects.

Managing Congregations Disorders

Much of what was said above about the management of individuals with personality disorders can equally be applied to pastors working with congregations that demonstrate a clear personality style. Like individuals, congregations are "true to type." They will function in ways to which they have been accustomed and that, to them, seem normal. An outsider, such as new pastor or a new visitor, might at first be taken aback by their strange behavior and be tempted to blame—either becoming angry at the congregation for its unusual and nonproductive behavior or becoming angry at themselves for being caught up in the congregational dynamics and acting in uncharacteristic ways. At such moments, it is wise to take a step backward. Instead of reacting to specific individuals who seem to be the source of the problems, consider the congregation as a whole: the silent, largely voiceless members as well as the noisy ones. It may at times become difficult to love specific individuals within a congregation, but pastors must be able to love the congregation they serve. If not, they can no longer minister in that place. What kind of personality do you perceive when you consider the whole? What is that personality's basic need? What is the best way to respond to that need? What is the best way to love it?

Difficult Pairings

Individuals with personality disorders appear to have a "fatal attraction" to certain other types of disordered personalities, as these relationships serve to create the kinds of disruptions and conflict that confirms them in their outlook on life. For example, narcissists are frequently drawn to other narcissists to form cliques of the special and unique, or they are drawn to dependents who will provide them with a constant supply of admiration. Borderlines are often fatally attracted to avoidants, as they most certainly will experience the abandonment they expect, while avoidants, for their part, find their belief that the world is tumultuous and an emotionally unsafe place reinforced by the instability of borderlines. Schizoids are attracted to histrionics for the drama they create, while histrionics find schizoids a challenging and difficult audience to impress. Dependents find that obsessive-compulsives are more than willing to make decisions for them while confirming their sense of their own inadequacies, while dependents provide obsessive-compulsives a relatively reliable environment that does not disturb their need for order and predictability. Antisocials delight in the trust and relative naiveté that avoidants and dependents provide, which makes them ripe for manipulation.

Paranoids are often drawn to obsessive-compulsives, as both share a need for perfectionism that is never satisfied.

In a similar manner, congregations with a certain personality style are often drawn to pastors with a certain kind of personality defect that will ultimately lead to problems. For this reason, during the "matchmaking" time, when pastors are appointed or are called to serve a new congregation, it is important for all involved to have some awareness of styles and the types of pairings that will prove to be the most detrimental. The choices that congregations and pastors make when engaged in the calling process are not always fully conscious or rational. Often, it is much like dating, where one's true self is carefully concealed in order to avoid rejection. When a congregation is in need of a pastor, it is usually because the previous pastor has left. If he or she was a beloved pastor, the congregation feels abandoned. If he or she was a despised pastor, the congregation is eager to prove that the problems that arose were all their former minister's fault, not theirs. When pastors seek a call, likewise, it is often because they felt unwanted or unappreciated in their former call. Thus, the situation is ripe for fantasy and self-deception, and the personalities of both are at work, sometimes leading to pairings that will confirm the worst features of each. It is prudent for pastors especially to be aware of their own personality traits and to be knowledgeable of their needs and inclinations that most likely lead to fatal attractions.

20 INTERIOR DESIGN FOR THE ARK

While camping at a state park in Arkansas, I noticed a flier announcing that the park ranger that evening would be giving a talk about the snakes of Arkansas at the park amphitheater. It was something to do, so we went.

I figured I might learn something about the snakes I already knew a little about, like copperheads, cottonmouths, and rattlesnakes (bad snakes) as well as perhaps king snakes and black snakes (good snakes). I was astounded when the presentation went on for more than an hour, detailing all of the thirty-six varieties of snakes found in Arkansas. Many of them were quite beautiful, with distinctive colors and geometrical markings and interesting behavioral characteristics. Only six of them were venomous, and even these, we were informed, were not as dangerous as commonly believed. Only seven people per year on average in the entire United States die from snake bite. You are more likely to die from falling out of bed, the ranger happily informed us, than from an encounter with a poisonous snake.

Still, as it was quite dark as we made our way through the forest from the amphitheater back to our campsite, one couldn't help but wonder how many of thirty-six species of slithery things might be lying there in the darkness all around us. We watched our steps very carefully.

The presence of personality disorders in congregations has led many to become wary of church environments as if they were places habituated by snakes. Seemingly without warning, one can find oneself criticized, judged, and attacked for apparently no reason other than that one had unwittingly become, in some manner, threatening. That many of the inhabitants of congregations, including those with certain forms for personality disorders, may be nonthreatening, intriguing, and beautiful people in their own right, doesn't ameliorate the sense of danger one often feels. Thus, both pastors and parishioners have been abandoning congregations in large numbers. But like the fear of snakes, the danger may be overly exaggerated and irrational.

Congregations are first and foremost communities. Their very vitality depends on the degree of diversity present. From the early ages of the church, a congregation was compared to Noah's ark, a place where all of the diversity of creation could find refuge and shelter from the storms of the world. Traditional church architecture, in many cases, was designed to replicate the ark. The place where the congregation sits is traditionally known as "the nave," after the Latin word for ship.

In the biblical account of the flood, the pairs of animals entering the ark included not only of "every kind of bird" and "every kind of animal" but also "every kind of creature that moves along the ground" (Gen. 6:20), leaving no doubt that snakes were to be included in this menagerie.

But while the Bible goes into a great amount of detail about the dimensions and the design of the exterior of the ark, it tells us nothing about the interior, about how the Ark was equipped to house the great variety of animals. It does not require much imagination to realize that a row of cages, all of equal dimensions, would not suffice. Each pair of animals would have different needs and would require different structures for shelter and feeding. God created the structure. It was up to Noah—and those who now lead the church—to find the ways to care for and to manage the diversity contained within.

The first known use of the word *menagerie*, meaning a collection of wild or foreign animals, dates from 1676. It derives from the French word ménage, meaning "household," implying that it was an attempt to integrate the animals in a manner in which they would be living together, rather than caged and restrained. It referred to one of the first structures built by Louis XIV of France in the gardens of Versailles. Its prominent feature was a beautiful pavilion, around which was a walking path. Outside this path were the enclosures. Each enclosure had a house or stable at the far end for the animals and was bounded on three sides with walls. There were bars only in the direction of the pavilion.

These eventually evolved into zoological gardens—the word "zoo" being derived from the Greek word ζώη, "life." The methods for housing and display of these animals have evolved over time so that, while still providing appropriate boundaries and barriers to protect both animals and zoo visitors alike, there is much greater openness and opportunity for interaction.

It is a mistake to think of the ark of the church as simply an empty hull where all are invited to enter with no attention given to interior design, to structures designed to provide for differing needs, and boundaries designed to keep everyone safe. There is great beauty in the diversity of the church, but only when, as in zoological gardens, a great deal of attention has been given to provide a balance between openness and barriers. Such a congregation would presumably neither be a place that naively "welcomes all" with no stated expectations or methods of accountability, nor a place where certain types of individuals in both subtle and direct ways are made to feel unwelcome.

Congregations typically have few expectations for their members. There is an assumption that it would be nice if they were to show up now and then for worship services, and perhaps once a year they are reminded that it would be a good idea if they were to give regularly if they want to keep the doors open. Additional involvement is simply a matter of volunteering, and because there always seems to be a dearth of volunteers, if you are willing to put yourself forward, you can have almost any position in the church that you want. That's exactly the kind of loose-knit structure that makes congregations the ideal playground for individuals with personality disorders.

There is nothing wrong with having expectations. Jesus frequently challenged his followers. The Scriptures frequently challenge believers. The task of caring for the animals in the ark presumably was not Noah's alone, nor should the task of managing and caring for the individuals brought together in a congregation solely be the responsibility of the pastor. And management and care begin with stating the expectations for life together in this community.

Congregational behavioral covenants can be a useful tool for providing the type of structure that can enable people to creatively live together despite differences. Gil Rendle's book on this topic is *Behavioral Covenants in Congregations: A Handbook for Honoring Differences.* His sample covenant for a church staff is provided in Appendix B.

For years, cancer has been treated by attempting to destroy the cancerous cells. Patients have been subjected to surgery, which attempts to remove the cancerous growth from the body, to chemotherapy, which is toxic to cancer cells, and to radiation, which generates toxic molecules that break up the cancer cells' DNA, causing their demise. Unfortunately, these methods have had only a modicum of success, often only after inflicting a great deal of misery and suffering on the patient. Only recently have additional methods been tried: Rather than attempting to destroy the cancerous cells, what if they could be restored to a normal function? What if, through genetic modification, the mutated cells could be "transformed" and restored to a normal function. This is the approach that is now being explored for the treatment of AML, a form of leukemia, as well as other types of cancer. What if a similar approach could be employed to respond to difficult parishioners and pastors, one that would neither allow the problems they create to fester and grow nor one which sees the only solution as excision?

I was once told, "The reason that congregations fail to be transformative is that individuals must leave their real self at the door of the church." Sad to say, that is often true. There is often the sense that one must conform in order to be accepted. The church becomes not an ark of diversity but "whitewashed tombstones" to employ Jesus's description—the place where all differences must be painted over in order to put on an air of propriety. But that inevitably produces discomfort. As Basil Pennington in his life of Thomas Merton (*Thomas Merton, My Brother*) writes, "We are broken persons and live in broken communities in a state of brokenness. We are alienated from ourselves and from each other. We do not readily fit together. We are like a bunch of porcupines trying to huddle together for warmth who are always driven apart out of fear of the wound we can inflict upon each other with our quills."

When discomfort strikes, more often than not, it is as a result of an encounter with a personality disorder. When one experiences an immediate emotional reaction, the wisest response is to do nothing. Rather, go home and think about it. Consider the possibilities. Could this be the type of emotional reaction typically elicited by a certain personality style, inviting you to a role in a drama? If so, realize that the person you have encountered is simply being true to themselves and to what they know. It is your task to identify their needs, of which they may only be dimly aware, and to respond in ways that will be most helpful to them, often in a manner that they don't expect or anticipate. When it is possible and appropriate, discuss with other congregational leaders your concerns and observations and together with them devise a plan of action that will put some limits on inappropriate behavior in a manner that also shows respect for a person who is merely being true to type.

The rattlesnake said to the boy, "But didn't you know what I was when you picked me up?" The proper care of snakes revolves around knowing and understanding the unique characteristics of each snake. Likewise, the care of parishioners is enhanced by knowing their different characteristics and traits and developing a plan for providing each with both appropriate management and loving care.

APPENDIX A
BEHAVIORAL COVENANT EXAMPLE—FOR STAFF
(Reprinted by permission of Rowman and Littlefield from *Behavioral Covenants in Congregations: A Handbook for Honoring Differences* © 1999 Rowman and Littlefield)

We promise to value our ministry of leadership to our congregation as a team and to offer our primary loyalty to that team.

We promise to express criticism and negative feelings first to the person, not to others.

We promise to refuse to talk with a complainer until that person addresses the person she or he is complaining about.

We promise to maintain confidentiality in staff conversations and meetings.

We promise to explain clearly to people who bring staff complaints that we will be sharing the conversation with staff.

We promise to commit to processing information about personality differences among staff and to give feedback to one another in order to support strengths and to balance weaknesses.

We promise to openly discuss our personal strategies and investments in proposals being made.

We promise to accept the fact that disagreements are expected and are to take place behind closed staff doors; in public we present ourselves as a team.

APPENDIX B
Summary of Spiritual and Congregational Issues Related to the Ten Personality Disorders

Cluster A (odd, eccentric behavior)
Paranoid

Descriptive: Distrustful and suspicious. The motives of others interpreted as malevolent. May exaggerate trivial events and find hidden meanings.

Fears: The world is unsafe, and others often fail to see the dangers.

Typical congregational involvement: Frequently overly pessimistic and critical. Often in conflict with pastors and lay leaders.

Faith issues: Lack of trust in God and others.

Pastoral care: Be nonreactive and provide objective feedback.

Schizoid

Description: Passively detached. History of withheld warmth. Colorless. Shy. Quiet. Nothing to connect with. Restricted range of emotions in interpersonal settings. Not boring. Indirect communication. Abstract thinking. Often invisible.

Fears: Few.

Typical congregational involvement: Attracted to but want repeated invitations.

Faith issues: Understand the idea of God but often lack experience of the same.

Pastoral care: Recruit for fitting roles; provide affirmation.

Schizotypal

Descriptive: Eccentric. Superstitious. Odd speech pattern. Deficient in interpreting social clues. Inappropriate or constricted affect. Lack of close friends.

Fears: May be irrational.

Typical congregational involvement: Most congregations have a few.

Faith issues: Eccentric beliefs.

Pastoral care: Provide community.

Cluster B (dramatic and erratic)
Antisocial
Description: Aggressive; lack of a conscience (aware of consequences, but not of right/wrong); kiss those above, kick those below; lack of remorse.

Fears: Healthy fear lacking.

Typical congregational involvement: Seldom (church is for "losers") unless they see the opportunity for financial or material reward.

Faith issues: No one is trustworthy.

Pastoral care: Only possible when they experience defeat.

Borderline
Descriptive: A pattern of intense and unstable interpersonal relationships alternating between extreme idealization and devaluation. Instant friends and instant enemies and frequent switching of one to the other. Impulsive. Actively recruit supporters.

Fears: Abandonment and fear of being alone.

Typical congregational involvement: Polarizing.

Faith issues: Reliability of God.

Pastoral care: Set boundaries and limits.

Histrionic
Description: Empty core, like dependent but not passive. Play roles to maneuver, manipulate, and exert pressure to get what they want. Often expressed sexually or with difficult to diagnose physical ailments

Fears: Abandonment.

Typical congregational involvement: They create drama (crisis of the week)!

Faith issues: Difficulty with "letting go, letting God."

Pastoral care: Avoid complimenting attention-seeking behavior and affirm nonhistrionic characteristics.

Narcissistic
Description: Self-absorbed; lack of empathy; grandiose; conflict; manipulate environment to survive. Believes self to be "special" and likes to associate with other special or high-status people.

Fears: Empty self being exposed.

Typical congregational involvement: All about me. Unethical (rules don't apply). Will recruit others to make self look good but will become angry when others begin to get attention.

Faith issues: Tends to use God.

Pastoral care: Compliment when appropriate but be wary of unethical or nonempathetic behavior.

Cluster C (anxious, fearful behavior)
Avoidant

Description: Actively detached. Socially inhibited with feelings of inadequacy. Has history of rejection and hypersensitive to it. Fear of commitment. Deep sense of shame. Demands unlimited loyalty.

Fears: Rejection.

Typical congregational involvement: Frequent church changes.

Faith issues: Lack of self-worth. Avoidance of community.

Pastoral care: Protect from abuse. Promise little and do more.

Dependent

Description: Likeable; believe source of all good lies outside themselves; lack confidence in their own judgments (say "I'm sorry" a lot); noncompetitive; exhibit submissive or clinging behavior.

Fears: Abandonment.

Typical congregational involvement: Faithful members but require a lot of attention.

Faith issues: Desire clear-cut answers; difficulty accepting grace.

Pastoral care: Set limits; don't give answers.

Obsessive-compulsive

Description: Preoccupation with orderliness; perfectionism; majoring in minors; stingy; attempts to control others; difficulty completing tasks; workaholic.

Fears: Losing control.

Typical congregational involvement: Rule based; passion for ritual; dislike of change; miserly concern about congregational finances.

Faith issues: God as stingy. Control God by conforming.

Pastoral care. Explore "What is your God like?" Explore past losses.

ABOUT THE AUTHOR

Roger Kruger is a pastoral counselor at Grace Point in Omaha, Nebraska, where his primary clientele are professional church workers and their families. He is a graduate of Concordia Seminary in St. Louis and earned his DMin in pastoral counseling and psychotherapy from Garrett Evangelical Theological Seminary in Evanston, Illinois. He served congregations as a parish pastor in Arkansas and Colorado before doing clinical training. He has written articles for *Congregations* and for *Christian Century* and is also the author of the book *In Jars of Clay: Reflections on the Art of Pastoring* (2007). More about his work with pastors and congregations can be found at his website www.careforclergy.com.